TEACHER BURNOUT

Edited by Alfred S. Alschuler
with Jaqueline Carl, Robert Leslie,
Ingrid Schweiger, and Diann Uustal

nea PROFESSIONAL LIBRARY
National Education Association
Washington, D.C.

First Printing: August 1980
Second Printing: August 1981
Third Printing: February 1984
Fourth Printing: January 1985

Note

The opinions expressed in this publication should not be construed as representing the policy or position of the National Education Association. Materials published as part of the Analysis and Action Series are intended to be discussion documents for teachers who are concerned with specialized interests of the profession.

Library of Congress Cataloging in Publication Data
Main entry under title:

Teacher burnout.

(Analysis and action series)
Bibliography: p.
1. Teachers—Psychology. 2. Job stress.
I. Alschuler, Alfred S., 1939- II. Series.
LB2840.T4 371.1'001'9 80-14770
ISBN 0-8106-1680-7

Contents

Related educational materials by Alfred S. Alschuler:

Resolving Classroom Conflict Through Social Literacy: An Audio Workshop. Washington, D.C.: National Education Association, 1980.

School Discipline: A Socially Literate Solution. New York: McGraw-Hill Book Company, 1980.

PREFACE

Many teachers accept stress as a normal part of their daily lives. They don't realize it can be as insidious as cancer, slowly destroying their mental and physical health. The first goal of this book is to help teachers recognize the signs of stress in order to know when it is a problem. A certain amount of stress in teaching is inevitable. However, teachers respond to stress differently—sometimes in effective ways that lead to professional accomplishments, sometimes in ineffective ways that are self-destructive. The second goal of this book is to describe what teachers can do to reduce work-related stressors and to choose self-enhancing responses. A successful campaign against stress will benefit everyone associated with schools. In addition, recognizing the problem and its solutions will be helpful to nearly everyone under stress.

ALFRED S. ALSCHULER, JAQUELINE CARL,
ROBERT LESLIE, INGRID SCHWEIGER,
and DIANN UUSTAL, *Editors*
UNIVERSITY OF MASSACHUSETTS IN AMHERST

CAUSES, CONSEQUENCES, AND CURES: A SUMMARY

Alfred S. Alschuler

Mr. Johnson is in a perpetual rush. He walks at a run, speaks like an auctioneer, and interrupts people by finishing their sentences for them. His pace is audible in foot tapping and knuckle cracking. Because he tries to get everything done in an impossibly short time, Mr. Johnson lives in a chronic state of frenzy. He is three times more likely to suffer a heart attack than his calmer colleagues.

Ms. Lauer left school in the middle of the semester. She had been complaining of dizziness, headaches, and general fatigue. A shy person, Ms. Lauer worried about being attacked or robbed in school. At times she seemed disoriented and preoccupied. It was rumored that she had a nervous breakdown.

As Ms. Skorpen was driving to work, trying to remember whether she had brought an answer key with her, she ran a red light and was hit broadside by a pickup truck.

Everyone knows what Mr. Buffin will say. Having seen superintendents come and go almost as fast as special federal projects, he believes that "reasons" are propaganda and enthusiasm is the mark of a fool. After teaching for twenty years he has become the school's resident cynic. Too old to start a new career, Mr. Buffin is doing time until retirement. Recently he summarized his years of teaching: "I've survived."

Hard-working teachers exposed to prolonged stress in schools risk becoming neurotically frenzied, battle-fatigued, physically injured, or burned out. Willard McGuire, NEA president, recently sounded the battle cry to stop the mutilation of teachers' spirits (and too often their bodies as well):

> A major new malady has afflicted the teaching profession and threatens to reach epidemic proportions if it isn't checked soon. It has already stricken thousands of sensitive, thoughtful, and dedicated teachers. . . . It is teacher burnout—a condition that results from stress, tension, and anxiety in its victims. . . . The NEA is hopeful, however, that once the teacher burnout problem is articulated to the community, it will get the attention it

deserves. . . . Teachers need support from parents; school administrators; school boards; and civic, business labor, religious, and professional societies. If teachers don't get that support, the price may be more than society can afford to pay.[1]

At stake is the enhancement or crippling of teachers' desires to teach, to love children, and to develop themselves as human beings.

This short practical book is designed to help teachers recognize the signs of stress and take steps to reduce it. The first two sections contain partial descriptions of the problem and suggested solutions. The last section of the book, "Workshop Guide for Reducing and Preventing Teacher Burnout," is a practical application of the recommendations presented by the contributors. This introductory chapter summarizes the subsequent material by answering three questions: What are the causes? the consequences? and the cures?

THE CAUSES OF STRESS

Stress occurs when individuals believe the demands from the environment are more than they can handle. "Stress" could be a one-word definition of teaching. For the major part of the school day teachers are isolated from other adults, a working condition shared by few other professions. It is not possible to work in depth daily with as many as 150 students who have unique learning histories, personalities, problems, and potentials. Deadlines, bells, excessive paperwork, inadequate supplies are "givens" in most schools. Free periods are "free" in name only. Rest and recuperation must take second place to preparation and grading. In addition to these normal demands, teachers are harrassed, more or less, in every class. Student sniping takes many forms: talking, whispering, lipreading, note passing, asking plausible but diverting questions, insulting the teacher, complaining about assignments, pushing, brushing against, touching, or shoving or hitting other students, throwing things, walking around to visit other students or to sharpen pencils several times a period, requesting passes, making a veritable symphony of noises. As many as 30 to 60 such incidents each period require the momentary diversion of the teacher's attention. When PA announcements, tardy students, and role-taking are included in this list, typically less than 50 percent of class time is spent on learning during a period in which teachers are expected to teach from bell to bell. In many schools absenteeism (with its attendant problems of catch-up instruction and makeup assignments) runs from 30 to 50 per cent, constituting a classical boycott.

Some students attack the school in ways that amount to guerrilla warfare. Attacks on personal property (thefts, malicious mischief, and arson) cost as much as $590 million annually, including increased insurance costs, security guards, sophisticated electronic surveillance equipment, and the expense of repairs and replacements. That is equivalent to a vandalism tax of $13 levied for every public school student. The human toll from the guerrilla warfare is equally staggering. Each year over 52,000 (5 percent) of the nation's one million secondary school teachers are attacked, 10,000 of whom require medical treatment; 60,000 teachers (6 percent) are robbed; and every month 120,000 (12 percent) have something stolen.[2]

If these internal pressures from the workload and students were not enough to cause stress, numerous external pressures are exerted on schools: to mainstream students with special needs; to provide multicultural and bilingual education; to reduce expenses in a period of rapid inflation; to respond to the questions of parents, the concerns of supervisors, and the achievement objectives of school boards and administrators. Simultaneously, declining enrollments foreshadow the strong possibility of reductions in the teaching force, i.e., layoffs. Beyond such pressures on all teachers, there are usually one or more intense stresses in teachers' personal lives: death, accident, or illness of a family member; divorce; debts; trouble with in-laws; changes in living conditions and personal habits. Not surprisingly, then, the combination of these job-related and personal pressures makes *stress* the number one health problem of teachers.[3]

THE CONSEQUENCES OF STRESS

Human beings respond to stress in three basic stages.[4] In Stage 1, *alarm*, the body mobilizes for "fighting or fleeing." In Stage 2, *resistance*, the person combats the stressor by purposeful action, by attempts to reduce the stressor, or by a variety of coping tactics. Stage 3, *exhaustion*, is commonly known as burnout. By analogy, these three states are like diving into cold water. At first the body is "alarmed" by the seeming frigidity. Then it is able to swim for a period of time while its "resistance" to the cold remains adequate. Finally, if the water is too cold or the swimming too long, the swimmer becomes "exhausted."

After the first alarm of stress, the body reacts physiologically. Adrenaline pours into the blood speeding up the heart rate and blood pressure. As sugar increases in the blood, more "fuel" is available for energy.

As red cells flood the bloodstream, more oxygen is transported to the muscles and the brain. Breathing accelerates to supply additional oxygen and to eliminate carbon dioxide created by increased activity. Because blood ordinarily required for digestion is shunted to the brain and the muscles, digestion slows. Pupils dilate, improving vision. Blood clotting ability accelerates. Such a reaction appears to be an ancient physiological syndrome that once prepared cavedwellers to fight or flee in response to threats in their environment.

This physiological syndrome can aggravate a wide variety of symptoms: difficulty in sleeping or insomnia, upset stomach, ulcers, ulcerative colitis, headaches, migraines, chronic back pains, shortness of breath, asthma, fainting, fever, high blood pressure, diabetes, stuttering, skin rashes, menstrual problems, Graves disease, hyperuricemia, multiple sclerosis, atherosclerosis, arthritis, anxiety, and depression. At worst, when stress is chronic and severe, it can lead to illness, accidents, or death.

Before these extreme consequences occur, however, individuals use a wide variety of coping tactics to "resist" the stress and accomplish their goals. Sometimes people develop a frenzied lifestyle, or what Friedman and Rosenman call "Type A behavior," described later in this book.

If the coping tactics are not adequate, or if the stress is too great for too long a period, four visible psychosocial symptoms of exhaustion/burnout are likely to occur.[5]

1. Distance from students and colleagues
   - Spending as little time with them as possible
   - Referring to human beings in terms of a single characteristic—my slow readers
   - The M.A.S.H. Syndrome—joking about someone's problems
   - The petty bureaucrat response—dealing with people using formulas
   - Intellectualizing about the causes of problems but not empathizing with the person
   - Decreased contact, i.e., eye contact, standing farther away, shorter conversations
   - Placing barriers between worklife and homelife.
2. Emotional and physical fatigue

   Teachers express the feelings that they just don't care anymore about what happens as a result of their efforts. In addition to sleeping poorly, a variety of physical symptoms begin to appear.

3. Attitude shift to the cynical
   Teachers burning out begin to express cold, callous, or hostile feelings about others, often stating that the student or administrator deserves to have the problem.
4. Total disgust
   This is "terminal burnout," or what Alfred Bloch describes in a subsequent chapter as "battle fatigue": hostility or complete malaise, depression, drug and alcohol abuse, taking more and more time to get less and less done, and/or psychiatric breakdowns.

National statistics reflect the consequences of stress on teachers. According to Willard McGuire, "A recent Teacher Opinion Poll revealed that one-third of those teaching now wouldn't go into teaching if they could go back to college and start again. Only 6 out of 10 said they plan to remain in teaching until retirement—early or mandatory. The number of teachers with 20 years' or more experience has dropped by nearly half in the past 15 years."[6]

Teachers are not alone in experiencing stress. The U.S. Clearinghouse for Mental Health Information estimated that the productive capacity of workers was reduced by $17 billion by stress-related problems. National interest is evident in over 90,000 published articles, 1,000 completed research projects, and an additional 6,000 articles printed each year.[7] Sooner or later everyone experiences stress, to a lesser or greater degree.

THE CURES FOR STRESS

Most practical articles on stress contain a list of suggestions to carry out. Virtually all such activities are ways to implement six strategies for reducing stress. Simultaneously these strategies promote healthy individual development and vibrant living. They are as follows:

1. Prevent stress by being alert to early signs and by helping others.

Like any disease, stress is most effectively reduced when it is diagnosed and treated early. Ongoing collaboration with other teachers prevents several stresses from occurring (i.e., isolation, loneliness, and the belief that the individual teacher is the only one having problems). Other suggestions for reducing stress include the following:

- Conduct a stress management and prevention workshop.

- Make a practice of sharing your feelings with at least one other teacher every day.
- Look for signs of stress in other teachers.
- Be supportive of colleagues by means of strokes, warm fuzzies, hugs, positive feedback, or by the priceless gift of your complete attention for even a brief period of time.
- Develop "mutual assistance pacts" between two to five teachers for small or large problems, in or outside school.
- Create a buddy system for support and problem solving.
- Set up a teacher hotline or drop-in teacher-counseling center in your district.
- Identify expert teachers who are willing to advise or help colleagues, particularly first-year teachers, on a confidential basis.

As Maslach concludes in her article on burnout,[8] "Our findings show that burnout rates are lower for those professionals who actively express, analyze, and share their personal feelings with their colleagues. Not only do they consciously get things off their chests, but they have an opportunity to receive constructive feedback from other people and to develop new perspectives and understanding."

2. Reduce the stressors.

So long as environmental stressors continue, teachers will need to develop and use stress reduction techniques. One type of primary stress prevention is to identify and reduce, if not eliminate, the causes. Here are several possibilities mentioned in the literature.

- Conquer common stressors. (See the chapter by Alschuler in the second part of this book.)
- Reduce the student/teacher ratio.
- Learn to say no.
- Establish a job rotation system involving a number of teachers to shift regularly into and out of high stress responsibilities (for example, monitoring the lunchroom).
- Lighten the load and responsibilities *outside* school.
- Reduce the amount of meeting time (for example, using memos in place of announcements).
- Share a contract with another teacher, both working half-time in school and half-time elsewhere.
- Use volunteers—aides, parents, community resources.
- Move into a team-teaching situation.

- Take a "sick day"; stress is teachers' number one "health" problem.
- Take a leave of absence or sabbatical.

All these tactics may reduce either the amount of external pressure or the exposure to that pressure. The ultimate reduction in exposure is to quit the job. For your health, happiness, and continued development, changing to a new type of work may, at some point, be the wisest decision. As Harry Truman said, "If you can't stand the heat, get out of the kitchen." He might have added that there are many other interesting rooms in the house.

3. Change your perception of the stress.

What is challenging for one person may seem exceptionally difficult and stressful for another. And all of us have experienced days of operating effectively followed by days of feeling stress and anxiety when responding to the same types of pressure. Often it is possible to alter the experience of stress by changing the perception of the situation. The following techniques, for example, may be helpful.

- Set more realistic goals, those where your chances for success are between 30 and 70 percent.
- Recall your basic values and goals as a way of seeing the trivia and clutter in perspective.
- Recall the list of things you have to be thankful for.
- Recall your priorities and the "80/20 rule": 80 percent of what is most valuable can be obtained by completing the top 20 percent of the tasks facing you.
- Recognize your own limits. Don't put on Superman's or Wonder Woman's cape. You can't teach, help, cure everyone, or even anyone, *all* the time. There are no ultimate solutions to human problems.
- Clarify for yourself that you are not responsible for the existence of the stressor, but you can manage your response to it.
- Accept what you cannot change.

4. Manage your physiological state.

In part, stress is physical. Some of its most destructive conquences are physical. It is possible to intervene in the physiological process, however.

- Learn how to relax without drugs. (See the chapter by Benson.) For some people a long hot bath does the trick.

- Learn to control your pulse, tension levels, and brain waves using a biofeedback device.
- Get more sleep.
- Establish a decompression routine between work and home (for example: 10 minutes sitting in a park, a short walk, 30 minutes uninterruptedly reading the newspaper).
- Meditate.
- Take minivacations during the day. Put your feet up for five minutes, breathe deeply, and look out the window.
- Purge yourself, in private. Laugh, cry, yell, scream, beat pillows with tennis rackets, chop wood, run to exhaustion.
- Get into good physical condition.
- Eliminate all processed sugar and caffeine from your diet.

5. Improve your coping abilities.

An obvious method for dealing with pressures is to become more efficient in getting the job done. By contrast, in "terminal burnout" people take longer and longer to accomplish less and less. Some of the most frequent recommendations for improving efficiency include the following:

- Manage your time better. Make lists, assign priorities. (See Lakein's suggestions in "Twenty Ways I Save Time.")
- Get special training in a needed skill area—classroom discipline, mainstreaming, bilingual and multicultural education.
- Delegate, delegate, delegate—anything and everything you can.
- Concentrate on one thing at a time. The experience of stress is partially the feeling of being flooded by too many things at once.
- If you're bored, choose a new curriculum topic in which you have an interest, or change the decor of your room, or go where the action is, or seek out those colleagues who are most "alive." Turn stress into vitality as Forbes suggests in a subsequent chapter.
- Read good professional books.
- Get help from a colleague, a friend, or a professional helper.

Whether or not they are chosen to reduce stress, these activities are legitimate since they promote personal competence and professional accomplishments.

6. Counteract stress.

Some activities preclude stress. When involved in them, you are unable to feel stressed. To a great extent the specific activity is an individual matter. However, some general advice is possible.

- Develop a positive addiction—jogging, swimming, hiking. (See the chapter by Glasser.)
- Be good to yourself: go to a movie, buy some clothes, eat ice cream, visit a friend.
- Balance your work and recreation. Develop an absorbing hobby—ceramics, yoga, guitar playing, stamp collecting, organic gardening, beekeeping, whale watching.

These six strategies and many similar tactics are not cure-alls. A certain level of stress is a fact of existence and is essential for effecive functioning. When stress is excessive or prolonged, however, it becomes dysfunctional and dangerous. These strategies and tactics can reduce stress to healthy levels. At the same time they constitute a healthier, happier way of life which incorporates (1) collaboration and mutual support, (2) a situation more conducive to teaching and learning, (3) realistic self-appraisal with clear, working priorities, (4) greater self-management and a more pleasant state of physical being, (5) increasing professional competence, and (6) a full, balanced life.

REFERENCES

[1]Willard H. McGuire, "Teacher Burnout," *Today's Education* 68, no. 4 (November-December 1979):5.

[2]National Institute of Education, *Safe Schools—Violent Schools* (Washington, D.C.: Government Printing Office, 1977).

[3]Robert Sylwester, "Stress," *Instructor* (March 1977):72-76.

[4]Hans Selye, *Stress Without Distress* (New York: Signet Books, 1975).

[5]Christine Maslach, "Burned-out," *Human Behavior* (September 1976):16-22.

[6]McGuire, "Teacher Burnout," p. 5.

[7]Boyd Swent and Walter Gmelch, *Stress at the Desk and How to Cope Creatively*, Oregon School Study Council Bulletin 21, no. 4 (1977):3.

[8]Maslach, "Burned-out," p. 22.

Part One:
What It Is

BURNOUT

I used to care.
but I don't care much any more.
I used to care
That children had to sit still and be quiet
And read pages 9 to 17
And answer the odd-numbered questions at the end of the chapter;
But I don't care much any more.

I used to care.
That finishing the assignment is more important than learning the skill.
And getting the right answer is more important than understanding, and apologizing is more important than being penitent;
But I don't care much any more.

I used to wake up in the night
And think about ways to teach children
To set goals and work toward them,
To make decisions and live with the results,
To work together.
But there were those who felt threatened
And those who felt frightened
Because my classroom was different.
Parents did not understand.
They listened to the evil insinuations and the confidential criticisms.
Their protests overwhelmed my sand-based supports.
I used to care,
But I don't care much any more.

Now I say
Sit down
Be quiet
Read pages 9 to 17
No exciting ideas disturb my sleep.
I haven't had a complaint in over a year.
Nobody seems to care
That I don't care much any more.

AN INSTRUCTOR'S GUIDE TO MURPHY'S LAW

Duncan Long

Murphy's Law says, "If anything can go wrong, it will." There are many corollaries and related regularities. Among them:

1. Good students move away.
2. New students come from schools that do not teach anything.
3. The teachers' lounge will be in the worst room of the school. It will contain dusty furniture and one noisy mimeograph machine.
4. The shorter the working time, the more the mimeograph will malfunction.
5. The clock in the instructor's room will be wrong.
6. The school board will make a better pay offer *before* the teachers' union negotiates.
7. When the instructor is late, he will meet the principal in the hall. If the instructor is late and does not meet the principal, the instructor is late to the faculty meeting.
8. Children who touch the instructor will have scabies or bubonic plague.
9. When speaking to the school psychologist, the teacher will say "weirdo" rather than "emotionally disturbed."
10. Disaster will occur when visitors are in the room.
11. The time a teacher takes in explaining is inversely proportional to the information retained by students.
12. Students who are blind, deaf, and/or behavioral problems will sit at the back of the room.
13. Extra-duty nights will occur when the best shows are on TV.
14. The problem child will be a school board member's son.
15. The instructor's study hall will be the largest in several years. The administration will view the study hall as the teacher's preparation time.

---

16. Students who are doing better are credited with working harder. If children start to do poorly, the teacher will be blamed.
17. Extracurricular duties will take more preparation time than classes.
18. Clocks will run more quickly during free time. (This is also known as the Law of Varying Time.)
19. A meeting's length will be directly proportional to the boredom the speaker produces.
20. On a test day, at least 15% of the class will be absent.
21. If the instructor teaches art, the principal will be an ex-coach and will dislike art. If the instructor is a coach, the principal will be an ex-coach who took a winning team to the state.
22. A subject interesting to the teacher will bore students.
23. Murphy's Law will go into effect at the beginning of an evaluation.

HOW TO TELL A TYPE A FROM A TYPE B

Meyer Friedman, M.D., and Ray H. Rosenman, M.D.

From the very time we began to think that a particular behavior complex bore responsibility for an increased risk of coronary artery and heart disease, we have been developing and refining methods of identifying individuals characterized by such patterns. . . .

The following section is intended to help you determine for yourself whether you are a Type A or Type B personality. If you are honest in your self appraisal—and if you are actually aware of your own traits and habits—we believe that you will not have too much trouble accomplishing this. The details of the behavior pattern vary, of course, according to many factors—education, age, social position. But most of you will be able to spot yourselves. Incidentally, we have found that Type A persons are by and large more common, and that if you are not quite sure about yourself, chances are that you, too, are Type A—not fully developed, perhaps, but bad enough to think about changing. And after you have assessed yourself, ask a friend or your spouse whether your self-assessment was accurate. If you disagree, *they* are probably right.

You Possess Type A Behavior Pattern:

1. If you have (a) a habit of explosively accentuating various key words in your ordinary speech even when there is no real need for such accentuation, and (b) a tendency to utter the last few words of your sentences far more rapidly than the opening words. The vocal explosiveness betrays the excess aggression or hostility you may be harboring. The hurrying of the ends of sentences mirrors your underlying impatience with spending even the time required for your own speech.
2. If you *always* move, walk, and eat rapidly.

---

3. If you feel (particularly if you openly exhibit to others) an impatience with the rate at which most events take place. You are suffering from this sort of impatience if you find it difficult to restrain yourself from hurrying the speech of others and resort to the device of saying very quickly over and over again, "Uh huh, uh huh," or "Yes yes, yes yes," to someone who is talking, unconsciously urging him to "get on with" or hasten his rate of speaking. You are also suffering from impatience if you attempt to finish the sentences of persons speaking to you before they can.

   Other signs of this sort of impatience: if you become *unduly* irritated or even enraged when a car ahead of you in your lane runs at a pace you consider too slow; if you find it anguishing to wait in a line or to wait your turn to be seated at a restaurant; if you find it intolerable to watch others perform tasks you know you can do faster; if you become impatient with yourself as you are obliged to perform repetitious duties (making out bank deposit slips, writing checks, washing and cleaning dishes, and so on), which are necessary but take you away from doing things you really have an interest in doing; if you find yourself hurrying your own reading or always attempting to obtain condensations or summaries of truly interesting and worthwhile literature.
4. If you indulge in *polyphasic* thought or performance, frequently striving to think of or do two or more things simultaneously. For example, if while trying to listen to another person's speech, you persist in continuing to think about an irrelevant subject, you are indulging in polyphasic thought. Similarly, if while golfing or fishing you continue to ponder your business or professional problems, or if while using an electric razor you attempt also to eat your breakfast or drive your car, of if while driving your car you attempt to dictate letters for your secretary, you are indulging in polyphasic performance. This is one of the commonest traits in the Type A man. Nor is he always satisfied with doing just two things at one time. We have known subjects who not only shaved and ate simultaneously, but also managed to read a business or professional journal at the same time.
5. If you find it *always* difficult to refrain from talking about or bringing the theme of any conversation around to those subjects which especially interest and intrigue you, and when unable to accomplish this maneuver, you pretend to listen but really remain preoccupied with your own thoughts.
6. If you almost always feel vaguely guilty when you relax and do absolutely nothing for several hours to several days.
7. If you no longer observe the more important or interesting or lovely objects that you encounter in your milieu. For example, if you enter a strange office, store, or home, and after leaving any of these places you cannot recall what was in them, you no longer are observing well—or for that matter enjoying life very much.
8. If you do not have any time to spare to become the things worth *being* because you are so preoccupied with getting the things worth *having*.
9. If you attempt to schedule more and more in less and less time, and in doing so make fewer and fewer allowances for unforeseen contingencies. A concomitant of this is a chronic sense of time urgency, one of the core components of Type A Behavior Pattern.

10. If, on meeting another severely afflicted Type A person, instead of feeling compassion for his affliction you find yourself compelled to "challenge" him. This is a telltale trait because no one arouses the aggressive and/or hostile feelings of one Type A subject more quickly than another Type A subject.
11. If you resort to certain characteristic gestures or nervous tics. For example, if in conversation you frequently clench your fist, or bang your hand upon a table or pound one fist into the palm of your other hand in order to emphasize a conversational point, you are exhibiting Type A gestures. Similarly, if the corners of your mouth spasmodically, in tic-like fashion, jerk backward slightly exposing your teeth, or if you habitually clench your jaw, or even grind your teeth, you are subject to muscular phenomena suggesting the presence of a continuous *struggle*, which is, of course, the kernel of the Type A Behavior Pattern.
12. If you believe that whatever success you have enjoyed has been due in good part to your ability to get things done faster than your fellow men and if you are afraid to stop doing everything faster and faster.
13. If you find yourself increasingly and ineluctably committed to translating and evaluating not only your own but also the activities of others in terms of "numbers."

The characteristics above mark the fully developed, hardcore Type A. Many people properly classified as Type A exhibit these characteristics in a lesser degree, however. If you are a moderately afflicted Type A subject, for example, you rarely feel or display much hostility. Your aggressiveness, although in excess, has still not evolved into free-floating rancor. You do not bristle with the barely governable rage that seethes so often just below the surface of the personality of the full Type A person.

Similarly, your impatience is not of towering proportions. You may attempt to squeeze more and more events into smaller and smaller pieces of time at work but often you can avoid this practice in off hours. You do not feel that you have to propel your "bicycle" faster and faster to keep your balance once your business or professional day has ended. At such times, like fire wagon horses unharnessed after returning from a fire, you may become almost torpid. But again like fire horses, who used to neigh and stomp their hooves just as soon as they heard the first peal of the fire alarm bell, so you, on hearing the alarm clock in the morning, shed your indolence and begin to hustle, bustle, and resume your strife with time.

Nor as a moderate Type A are you *obsessively* involved in the acquisition of sheer numbers. You are still aware of the many nonnumerate, charming aspects of full-bodied, full-souled living, even if you cannot completely enjoy and lose yourself in them.

You Possess Type B Behavior Pattern:

1. If you are completely free of *all* the habits and exhibit none of the traits we have listed that harass the severely afflicted Type A person.
2. If you never suffer from a sense of time urgency with its accompanying impatience.
3. If you harbor no free-floating hostility, and you feel no need to display or discuss either your achievements or accomplishments unless such exposure is demanded by the situation.
4. If, when you play, you do so to find fun and relaxation, not to exhibit your superiority at any cost.
5. If you can relax without guilt, just as you can work without agitation

The Type B person is far more aware of his capabilities than concerned about what peers and superiors may think of his actions. Unlike the Type A person, who really is never quite certain of his virtues and cannot ever quite face up to his deficiencies, you as a Type B know fairly well the value of your virtues and have resigned yourself to the restrictions that your deficiencies set upon you. You seek and succeed in finding your self-confidence by a process of candid self-appraisal. The Type A man seeks but never quite succeeds in finding self-confidence because he looks for it in the acquisition of an ever-increasing set of "numbers."

You, too, may strive for the things worth having. Indeed, as the "tortoise" (which the Type A "rabbit" more or less always believes you are) you may, in the final stretch, obtain a greater share of the things worth having than your Type A counterpart. But usually (if you have not been too critically wounded by the ethos of our times) you also attempt to become at least some of the things worth being. In any event, you do not build your life's ladder with rungs composed solely of numbers.

You may not be a completely developed Type B, but if you are relatively free of all the habits enslaving the Type A subject, and if you exhibit relatively rarely any of his traits, then you may still be classed as a Type B. You may occasionally feel a sense of time urgency, but if you do, it will be associated exclusively with your vocational and never with your avocational activities. Also, even at work, you will not feel this stress except during those limited periods when the demands of your position make it logical to feel that time is short. For example, if you are an accountant, you may well feel a sense of time urgency during the first two weeks of April.

But precisely like a fully developed Type B person, you, too, never suffer from the presence of free-floating hostility nor do you habitually attempt to speed things up like a Type A. You, too, strive to acquire the things worth having, but again, you will not do so at the expense of totally disregarding the pursuit of the things worth being.

We have presumed to slice the spectrum of personality types rather sharply, and possibly, rather arbitrarily. Even in our increasingly standardized society, human beings possess personalities that cannot be nearly so precisely categorized as has been done here. Behavior types tend to run together to some extent. Then, too, there are some people (but no more than about 10 percent of an urban population) who possess some habits and exhibit some traits that are Type A and some that are Type B. Ordinarily, though, it is not difficult to recognize and differentiate persons with Type A Behavior Pattern from persons with Type B. . . .

In attempting to assess yourself, we should again like to suggest that before you make your final decision whether you are a Type A or B person, you request the advice and opinion of your spouse, or a relative or friend who knows you well. We have observed that many Type A persons are totally unaware of either the presence or effects of their behavior pattern. They do not notice their restlessness, their tense facial muscles, their tics, or their strident-staccato manner of speaking. Nor are they always aware of their free-floating hostility—when it is present—if only because they can rationalize it so beautifully. Some Type A persons are not even aware of their sense of time urgency; it has been present so long that it seems a part of their personality. For that matter, they may be understandably reluctant to recognize, as enslaving and spiritually devastating, habits and traits that only yesterday were held in high esteem by all—including Horatio Alger and his prosperous friends.

THE BATTERED TEACHER

Alfred M. Bloch, M.D.

In December 1974, John S., a 41-year-old teacher, entered the sound and control booth of an inner-city high school auditorium. As he closed the door, he confronted two male students who had been cutting the power lines and smashing electrical equipment. One of the students fled; the other began beating Mr. S. with his fists. When the student who had fled returned, he held John S., while the other grabbed a chair and began battering the teacher's head and shoulders. Mr. S's screams were unheard. The battering continued, and John S. finally lost consciousness.

During the 1975-76 school year, NEA estimates that some 63,000 classroom teachers were physically attacked by students. In a survey of incidents on public school property, the Senate Juvenile Delinquency Subcommittee reports that between 1970 and 1973 murders increased 19 percent; rapes, 40 percent; robberies, 37 percent; and assaults on teachers, 77 percent. This year, as in recent years, thousands of teachers will be threatened, harassed, and physically assaulted on campus. They will become aware of their personal danger and vulnerability. They will become fearful and develop stress-related symptoms that will affect them psychologically and physically.

Between 1971 and 1976, I evaluated 250 classroom teachers (and treated some of them) who had symptoms of either physical trauma and/or prolonged psychic stress. They were referred to me by other physicians, attorneys seeking workmen's compensation for their clients, and fellow teachers. Most of them did not return to campus; they are on disability as a result of the physical and/or mental harassment they suffered on their jobs.

These teachers, White, Black, Mexican American, Asian American, had all taught in inner-city schools within the Los Angeles Unified School District for periods of time ranging from two months to 14 years. All had experienced, on campus, the physical and psychic trauma of beatings; assaults with weapons; or continued harassment and threats of violence from students, parents, and vagrants. All presented symptoms of anxiety, fear, and depression. Many presented psychophysiological manifestations of prolonged stress (e.g., migraine headaches, ulcers, hypertension).

Many of the psychological symptoms of these teachers were similar to those of people who have suffered from "combat neurosis" and of survivors of war disasters (e.g., emotional tension, anxiety, insecurity, nightmares, excessive startle response, phobias, cognitive impairment, blurred vision, dizziness, fatigue, and irritability). Their physical symptoms, also similar to those of combat neurosis, ranged from headaches and skin disorders to peptic ulcers, hypertension, and respiratory problems.

The teachers who have presented symptoms comparable to combat neurosis are the battered teachers of this report. Ironically, during interviews, many referred to their schools as "battle zones."

The following three case studies from the group of teachers I treated illustrate reactions to traumatic events and the effects of prolonged stress. After a teacher has been physically attacked or repeatedly threatened, he or she develops fear and anxiety. When this state is prolonged or aggravated and the school administrators offer little or no support or protection to the teacher, the teacher experiences psychological and physical depletion and ultimately collapses.

Case 1. Howard K., a 47-year-old teacher, had been assigned to an inner-city high school between 1960 and 1974. He had been physically well and had enjoyed his work until about the eighth year of his assignment, when, he said, school morale and discipline deteriorated and campus violence and vandalism increased markedly.

Despite the danger of trying to stop heated disputes on campus, Mr. K., who believed that personal risks were secondary to maintaining order, intervened in fights. On one occasion when he tried to stop a fight, participants and onlookers as well severely beat him. Subsequently, he became the target of several physical assaults by students, some of whom were members of juvenile gangs. Then, when Mr. K. attempted to prevent a student from stealing school equipment, the student drew a knife and threatened to kill him. Mr. K. reported the boy to the administrative office. The student was suspended from school for three days. When he returned, he renewed his threats to murder Mr. K.

A few weeks later, Mr. K. was surprised to find a door to the auditorium unlocked after school hours. As he opened the door, a metal chair and desk came crashing down from the balcony and missed him by inches. An investigation revealed that a booby trap had been set to be activated when that door opened.

Approximately six years ago, Mr. K. was depressed and "moody." He became easily fatigued and had difficulty climbing stairs without experiencing pain in his leg. His physician diagnosed the pain as "psychological." The pain worsened, and Mr. K. began to experience severe leg pain after walking short distances. When the pain increased to a level he described as "intolerable," he consulted another physician, who diagnosed the problem as atherosclerosis of the major arteries of his legs, a stress-related disease. A surgical replacement of these atherosclerotic vessels with Teflon "arteries" was performed with good results.

Mr. K. sustained his last beating from a student in February 1974. Despite continued requests for transfer to another school, he was not given a new assignment. There was no exit!

To date, he continues to suffer psychological symptoms of depression (e.g., fatigue, nightmares and insomnia, damaged self-esteem, irritability). He is unable to function in many capacities. He has not returned to teaching.

Case 2. I evaluated Ms. R., a 31-year-old high school teacher, in November 1975. She was hospitalized in December 1975 after a suicide attempt.

She had successfully taught continuation classes for six years in Northern California, because, she said, the school administrator had given teachers strong support and had protected the staff. When a knife-wielding student threatened to "cut up" her face in 1972, she was able to escape and to run for help. The administrator handled the situation so well that she sustained little or no psychological sequelae from this trauma and returned to school the next day.

When she began teaching at a Los Angeles inner-city school, however, her classroom and facilities, designed to accommodate 22 students, had an enrollment of 30. Within weeks, her class enrollment had swelled to 56. Many of these were "problem" students.

Students in her class harassed and threatened her. She saw violence directed toward other teachers at this school. Although she reported only the threats that were directed toward her to the school administration, she was offered neither psychological support nor physical protection. All requests to reduce her class size or provide additional personnel or facilities were ignored or denied.

The patient became progressively more anxious and depressed. After completing two months of this teaching assignment, she was passing out report cards when a group of female students, angry about their low grades and recorded absences, gathered around her and set her hair on fire. Others present in the room helped put out the fire. Afterward, when she attempted to report this incident to the school principal, she was criticized for leaving the classroom and for not maintaining discipline among her students. In addition, she was instructed not to discuss the assault with her fellow teachers. She became agitated, anxious, and severely depressed. She has been unable to return to teaching.

Case 3. Mr. F., 29 years old, was a high school teacher who was popular among the students. On an especially hot and humid afternoon, he held his afternoon class outside on the campus lawn in the shade. During the class, three males, none of whom were students at the school, walked into the circle of students. Mr. F. asked, "May I help you?" Without responding, the three grabbed Mr. F., threw him on his back, and then kicked and beat him until he lost consciousness.

Mr. F. was treated at the hospital for facial, mouth, and gum lacerations. Some of his teeth had been knocked loose. When told of the incident by telephone, the principal advised Mr. F. to return to class the next day to "show the students that violence had not won."

Since this assault, Mr. F. has developed many physical complaints and experiences episodes of anxiety and paranoia. He has nightmares and suffers from fatigue. Formerly an "all around" college athlete, he was a dedicated and idealistic teacher, and though he has not left the profession, he is actively seeking alternative employment.

Case 1 illustrates the effects of physical trauma and prolonged stress on a teacher who experienced a psychological and psychophysiological breakdown. Case 2 illustrates a more acute psychological breakdown as the result of stress and physical trauma. Case 3 illustrates psychological depletion immediately following physical trauma. These three cases substantiate the fact that continued stress cannot be sustained indefinitely without symptoms of psychological and/or physiological depletion. These patients represent the new form of combat neurosis—the battered teacher.

During my interviews with these 250 teachers, only two of whom had had previous psychiatric treatment, they pointed out the following problems:

- *Psychological and somatic complaints*. They reported somatic illnesses; they complained of fatigue and weakness, blurred vision, irritability, sensitivity to weather, difficulty in coping, dizziness, malaise, and depression.

Their specific complaints represented the full range of stress-related illnesses. Cardiovascular symptoms included palpitations, hypertension, arteriosclerosis, and coronary artery disease. Musculoskeletal symptoms included back difficulties, cervical tension, headaches, etc. Respiratory symptoms included repeated upper respiratory infections and bronchial asthma, hyperventilation, etc. Some teachers had evidence of physical trauma: lacerations, bruises, etc., as well as head injuries, seizures, and deafness.

• *Anxiety concerning the continuum of campus violence.* These teachers reported that the violence aimed at them included direct threats of murder and rape, actual physical assault and injury by students with and without weapons, theft, arson, and various other forms of vandalism of personal property. Violence on campus not specifically directed at them included bombings of classrooms, theft and destruction of campus equipment, fights between students and gang members, murder, and rape. They said that open-locker searches on some of their campuses revealed drugs, dynamite, knives, stilettos, ammunition, rifles, and handguns.

The presence of gang members, vagrants, and nonstudents on campus has continued to plague inner-city schools as a major problem contributing to violence. Many battered teachers reported that neither the administration nor security personnel are able to control the presence or actions of anonymous vagrants.

These teachers described the combination of gang warfare and the presence of weapons on campus as volatile. One teacher told of a gang member who, recently transferred from another school and assigned to his metal shop class, felt obliged to kill a student of an opposing gang whom he spotted in the same class. The first student, exasperated because his intended victim had failed to attend school that day, took out a pistol and fired two clips of ammunition into the classroom and school office before staff members subdued him. Security personnel were not immediately available, because they were concurrently investigating a stabbing incident that had occurred in another area of the same campus.

• *Lack of preparedness.* These teachers indicated they were unprepared to cope with school violence, especially when gang warfare and weapons were involved. They were not prepared physically or psychologically to be the focus of threats and physical assault. Therefore, they relied on others to protect them (e.g., security officers or the administration). When disillusioned by their vulnerability and helplessness and the absence of protection or support from the administration, they became anxious and fearful. This phenomenon was reinforced with continued incidents of violence.

Whatever their initial motivation had been for teaching, none had received "basic training" to prepare them for the violence they encountered in "combat zones."

• *Difficulty in reporting incidents.*

1. Many said administrators made them feel responsible for being the targets of violence. This they said was the most demoralizing aspect of reporting

incidents. When this happened, they felt outrage, and because they were unable to strike back, they experienced lowered self-esteem. For example, after Mr. K. (Case 1), who is White, sustained a 15-minute battering from an angry Black student wielding a chair, his principal told him, "This [incident] is *your* fault and reflects *your* inability to communicate with the minorities."

2. These teachers said the number of psychological assaults (threats, harassments, intimidation) greatly exceeded the number of physical assaults, but they were not considered reportable.

3. Although legally required to report incidents of violence, these 250 teachers were often discouraged from doing so. Frequently they stated that school administrators gave them the implicit message that it was "not in their best interest" to report an incident. As a result, these teachers tried to function under a Damoclean sword: the threat to their job security if they were "unsuccessful teachers" and the continued ordeal of facing violence in their classrooms and on campus.

4. Some of these teachers also said that in an attempt to keep out vagrants, their schools required that classroom windows and doors remain locked during class and opened only at the end of class. Because most intercommunication systems either were in disrepair or had been stolen, teachers who were threatened by violence during a class period had no way to communicate for help.

• *Overcrowded classrooms*. These teachers reported that their classes had as many as 75 percent more students than they should have had. Many contained violence-prone students who had police records.

• *Poor leadership and ultimate breakdown of morale*. Teachers who had received little or no support after sustaining injuries or being threatened stated that they believed the school administrators were more concerned with projecting an acceptable profile than they were with the safety of the teaching staff. (I must emphasize that these teachers consistently stated that if their schools had had adequate security measures and if their administrators had been supportive, they could have continued with their teaching assignments. One woman in this series, who had been violently beaten by a student, had the full and sympathetic support of her school principal; after recovering from her physical wounds, she returned to teaching and is doing fairly well.)

• *Difficulty in obtaining transfers out of stressful areas*. Teachers' requests for transfers to other schools in less stressful areas were usually denied. The added frustration of no escape from an intolerable situation short of resignation seemed to effect symptoms of final breakdown. Somatic and psychological complaints increased until the battered teacher became physically and psychologically disabled.

- *Predisposing factors.*

1. An impaired ability to deal effectively with fear or danger was the primary predisposing factor present in more than 75 percent of the teachers I treated. Results of the Minnesota Multiphasic Personality Inventory (MMPI) and projective tests of these teachers indicated they are obsessional, passive, idealistic, dedicated persons, who are unable to understand or cope with the violence directed toward them. When they were the targets of violence or hostility, they were unable to strike out or retaliate and internalized their rage and fear. (Military personnel with this same personality structure comprised more than 15 percent of the psychiatric casualties of World War II. Their levels of anxiety and depression were usually high, and they tended to focus upon physical symptoms of their anxiety, e.g., heart palpitations, headaches, gastrointestinal disorders.)
2. Many of these teachers had an attitude of defeatism caused by poor leadership. Those from schools where administrative support was inadequate reported low school morale and a high incidence of psychological and physical complaints among the faculty. The same phenomenon was observed in war studies. Leadership and total support are as vital to good morale of teachers in "combat zones" as to military personnel in combat situations.

As indicated above, the battered teachers of this series have shown the same correlation between incidence of their symptoms and factors of stress as military personnel suffering from combat neurosis.

Military personnel, however, know that upon completion of a combat mission or upon surviving for a certain period of time in a war zone, they will be rotated to a nonstressful place for rest and recuperation before being returned. Studies show that this procedure has a positive effect on their adverse physical symptoms.

Treatment for military psychiatric casualties includes rest, sedation, ventilation of anxieties, abreactions and narcosis, followed by rapid return to the front. Treatment for teachers who present symptoms of trauma or continued stress, however, is usually disallowed until they collapse from complete physiological or psychological depletion. There are administrators who simply dismiss them as "unsuccessful teachers."

Teachers can survive in stressful schools if proper procedures are intiated. The essential measures of prevention and control of stress and trauma are as follows:

1. *Preparedness.* Psychological and physical training for the stressful situation

is crucial for the survival of these teachers. Such training could minimize the impact of violence on them.

2. *Crisis intervention teams*. Crisis intervention units should be available in each school district. They would consist of two or more empathic teachers with mental health training and experience who would immediately go to the aid of the battered teacher. Of course, persons who sustain an attack may need additional psychiatric treatment to diminish the posttraumatic effects.

3. *Morale*.

- The teaching staff must have the support of school board members and administrators.
- Personal security should be guaranteed to each teacher while on the school grounds.
- While assigned to inner-city schools with high violence profiles, teachers should receive hazard pay or some other compensation.
- After attacking a teacher or any other member of the staff, violent students should not be allowed to return to the same classroom. Too often, after a short absence, these students return to school as heroes. I recommend their suspension for longer periods.
- The three R's—rotation, rest, and recuperation from the combat zones—should be afforded the teachers, i.e., at the end of a maximum two- or three-year period, the teachers should be rotated to a less stressful school.
- Classroom teachers should have an opportunity to report *directly* to the school board about unfair administrators, overcrowding, violence, etc. This would be constructive in that teachers will know that "someone is listening," and that when needed, remedial measures may be taken.

4. *Sharing*. Teachers should have the oportunity "to share" or "to work through" the violent events that they encounter. Working through at the individual and group level is an important aspect of the ultimate acceptance of the event and its consequences. This should relieve some of the teacher's psychic load and facilitate the development of good morale. Sharing will relieve tension and help develop camaraderie among members of the teaching staff.

Part Two:
What to Do About It

HOW SOME TEACHERS AVOID BURNOUT

Andrew J. DuBrin, Jerry Fowler, Larry Hoiberg, James E. Mathiott, Faye Morrison, Peggie Case Paulus, Elizabeth Prince, Sandy Stein, and Bettie Burres Youngs

You've had it, you say! Simply getting up in the morning and dragging yourself to school is agony. You're dissatisfied with your work, depressed, exhausted. You're suffering from career claustrophobia and you find yourself screaming inwardly, "Let me out!" You are, in short, a victim of teacher burnout. You are not alone. Teacher burnout is a debilitating disease, caused by a number of bugs—lack of mobility, less turnover on teaching staffs, public scrutiny of schools, media assault, budget reversals, you name it. But there are cures, and they work. *Instructor* went in search of them, talking with psychiatrists, counselors, and teachers themselves. We found them. If your flame's dying, here's the fuel you need. . . .

Kindergarten teachers in Northeastern Colorado have organized KIDS (Kindergarten Instructional Development Society). They hold a mini-workshop once every two months in different areas of their state. Meetings start promptly at 6 P.M. and end at 9 P.M. Each teacher brings one idea to share with the others. Topics include math games, science, fairy tales, puppets, reading, and so on. "It's a tremendous way to keep excited about teaching," says Hilda Barelman, one of the organizers.

Make ten vows to freshen your act. What do veteran teachers do to keep fresh, excited, and wide-eyed about teaching? Peggie Case Paulus suggests these ten commandments. Raise your right hand and read aloud:

I. Keep alert to changing methods and philosophies.

II. Attend conferences, workshops, and in-service programs with an open mind.

III. Listen to other teachers in your school.

IV. Avoid like the plague the stereotype of talking only about school after hours.

V. Keep alert physically and mentally.
VI. Keep in step with students and find out about their hobbies, movies, and music.
VII. Discard . . . discard . . . discard old ideas, old prejudices, old materials.
VIII. Read more than "Dick and Jane" books and subscribe to professional magazines.
IX. Be flexible and avoid doing something just because it's always been done that way.
X. Keep your senses sharpened, your mind keen, and your heart open to remain an enthusiastic teacher! *Peggie Case Paulus*

Shake your career stagnancy blues. Making a career change is one way to overcome malaise. But reflecting on why you went into teaching, discovering new strengths within yourself, is an effective, and probably more practical, alternative. Consider what motivates you. Is it money? Control over your life? Feeling significant to others? Inner fulfillment? Answer these questions and perhaps you'll be on the road out of career stagnancy. Check each box getting a *yes* answer.

☐ Are you enjoying your career?
☐ Are you getting the most out of life?
☐ Do you use your potential?
☐ Are you making the best use of your time and skills?
☐ Do you value productive work?
☐ Are you happy teaching?

If you checked fewer than three boxes, answer the following:

1. Why did you go into teaching?
2. What positive attitudes did you feel when you first began?
3. Have those attitudes changed? Why?
4. What activities in teaching are most satisfying?
5. What are the settings and skills you use in those activities?
6. What activities are least satisfying?

Now, determine how you can change those activities you dislike and improve those activities you enjoy. *Bettie Burres Youngs*

How do experienced teachers keep going? What suggestions do they have for you?

Tom Bernagozzi, Bay Shore, New York: Get away summers. I've taken study tours to England and Spain. When possible get away weekends, too.

When getting stale, sit down with friends who teach to design a new unit. Attend and give workshops. I find creating my own musicals with third graders stimulating also.

Bob Bisson, White Plains, New York: Get involved with things outside of school—organic gardening, bee colonies, peanut growing. Don't get tied down to somebody else's program. Keep in touch with people who are alive and moving ahead. And make changes: Twelve years ago, I went to Africa for two years. This year I switched to a new school, which is invigorating.

Glennellan Brun, Eugene, Oregon: Take a leave of absence. After nine years of teaching, I'm pursuing a Ph.D. to renew my energies and do more in-depth reading.

Dean Kindig, Rochester, New York: Get away from it all. Driving out west last summer with my wife annd camping high in the mountains got me over my seven-year itch. I plan to keep this spirit alive by forming an Adventure Club for adults; by bicycling; by staying close to the cutting edge.

Kathy Nelson, Redwood City, California: One way to avoid burnout is to go on a shared-contract with another teacher. I just had a baby and I work halftime with another special ed teacher. It's a good way to keep professionally active without burning out.

EVER CONSIDER A SABBATICAL?

Many teachers are failing to take sabbaticals, the traditional safeguard against burnout, according to officials at NEA. While funds have been cut in some areas, they still exist in many others. Contact your local administration or union to see if you might be eligible. What could you do? Mena Topjian, first-grade teacher in Lexington, Massachusetts, traveled from Alaska to Argentina studying Native American groups. A Brattleboro, Vermont, third-grade teacher studied minimum competencies in her state. Write curriculum groups, organizations, exchange programs, travel programs, state departments of education, federal grant-giving agencies, and so on to cook up your own year away from it all.

Take a year's leave of absence. Julie and Larry Fuhrman Davis, Youngstown, Ohio, retired for a year. They had saved their money and made a few sound investments; so they spent their time entertaining, camping, traveling, and skiing. After ten years of teaching, they felt they needed a change. They returned to teaching recharged.

THESE SCHOOLS HELP SAVE TEACHERS

At Rockford Elementary School, Minnesota, Principal Robert Ziegler has *teachers switch grades* periodically It breaks up routines, provides new challenges, and reinforces the adage, "variety is the spice of life."

Sandy Stein, a former therapist in Madison, Wisconsin, conducted an in-service course, Hugging Helps. A hug is any kind of positive feedback ("You gave that lesson well") and she believes it helps prevent burnout.

"Some psychologists feel that those who survive burnout are the ones who've learned to pace themselves and withstand stress," Stein notes. "I think that what causes burnout is the negative reinforcement people get—as in, 'You're five minutes late'—rather than an affirmation for what they're doing that's creative, innovative, or right." The Hugging Helps course reminds people that it's okay to compliment yourself and others; the sessions teach people how to do it.

Another in-service course popular in Madison is Choosing, Changing, Recharging Your Career. And the principal in one of the system's districts has organized an Employee Assistance Program and an Employee Health Program for *all* his employees.

Supervisors in Grand Forks, North Dakota, have taken the offensive against the pressure on teachers for accountability and designed a *five-step observation program* to help teachers improve their teaching. The teachers themselves decide what they want to accomplish in class and when. Supervisors meet with teachers before and after the observations, giving positive feedback and suggestions for improvement. *Larry Hoiberg*

A friend, a helper, a guide . . . that's what new teachers get in the Orleans Parish School System in New Orleans during the crucial first two years of teaching. They can call confidentially one of eight *teacher advocates* for help with curriculum and discipline problems. Advocates also work with teacher selection committees and provide in-service workshops The program has paid off—there have been fewer resignations and teachers feel the system cares. *Elizabeth Prince*

A *Floating Faculty* of 19 master teachers and one principal recharges teachers in Prince George's County, Maryland. Since teachers have fewer opportunities to interact with their peers than those in other professions, the FF spends two weeks in a school, providing practical assistance in implementing reading competency strategies. During the first three days, the team replaces classroom teachers so they can attend workshops Then one member of a faculty is paired with a fellow professional for other workshops and demonstrations. Teachers feel it improves more than their reading instruction. It generates new ideas and fires up a school. *Jerry Fowler*

Project Reenew (Renewing Enthusiastic Employment in Education Work) gives employees grants for special projects in Palo Alto, California. Part of the $24,000 budgeted in 1977 went to release a teacher from her class to write a unit on the King Tutankhamen exhibit before it arrived in the area. Another grant went to staffs from two schools to plan year-long, staff-development meetings. And a teacher with an outstanding reading program became a demonstration teacher for others in nearby schools.

The project also has a Personal Help Center where district counselors are available for short-term, confidential consultations, which in some cases have saved careers.

Another positive practice in Palo Alto is the releasing, each year, of one classroom teacher to plan curriculum activities around a textbook adoption in one of five basic subject areas. After this special assignment, the teacher returns to the classroom professionally renewed. *James Mathiott*

Many teachers and schools have devised seemingly simple ways to avoid burnout.

1. One teacher hires older students to do routine clerical work, stays late at school finishing her work before leaving the building, takes a short nap at noon to restore her energy, and finds a staff "buddy" each year.
2. Others jog before or after school or at noon. It limbers the bodies, renews spirits, and calms nerves.
3. If parent conference schedules are impossible, your school may want to restructure your school week as teachers in some areas have done. They begin school 15 minutes earlier to meet the required instructional minutes and have one minimum day per week for parent conferences and curriculum planning.
4. Teachers driven to distraction by working individually with beginning reading students find it more relaxing to work a longer day! By having half their students come early and leave early and half come late and leave late, they have reading groups twice a day.
5. Morning bulletins in each teacher's box can cut down on staff meetings, frequently a drain at the end of the day.
6. Some faculties plan a yearly fall retreat to meld personalities and to set a focus for the school year (or in the early spring, to redirect energies for the year). These sessions help teachers work cooperatively and avoid stress.
7. A "Good Times" party in the spring can be just for parents and teachers. Precede a potluck dinner and dance with small preparty gatherings in various homes, mixing teachers and parents.

8. Older teachers—tired but not ready to step out of teaching entirely—may elect a preretirement plan in many sections of the country. From age 50, teachers may elect to work 20 to 30 days a year in the school at a professional task mutually acceptable to teachers and administration. Remuneration varies from 30 to 50 percent of salary depending on the plan chosen, and it can go as long as five years. *Faye Morrison*

WHAT CAN EDUCATION LEARN FROM INDUSTRY?

Dr. Mortimer Feinberg has seen many a depressed, burned-out executive. As an industrial psychologist, he has worked with the nation's largest corporations. We wondered just how he'd treat burned-out elementary teachers.

"First, we have to determine if the depression is internalized," he said. "If you have trouble sleeping, no appetite or sexual drive, emotional bursts of anger, you probably have internalized kinds of problems and need professional counseling. Maybe the solution is retirement or changing jobs.

"But, if you're perfectly happy away from your job, then you know that it is an external problem and your job is getting to you. For these people, we can do something.

"The mind is like a tire. If it isn't rotated, it is going to wear out faster. To rotate the mind, don't have it constantly in the same gear. Maybe switch assignments for a year, kindergarten this year, fourth grade next. But also go beyond that. Spend your leisure time with adults. Do something different evenings and summers.

"It's important to build self-esteem. Many industries have adopted the Japanese practice of a godfather—placing a person in charge of newer employees to inspire or teach, to act as a guardian. Schools could, and should, adopt this practice.

"There are other ways to build esteem. For example, everyone has some expertise or specialized talent. If the word went out that Ms. .... was going to conduct a workshop on her talent—casserole cooking, the Constitution of the U.S., macrame, whatever—after school on Tuesday, other teachers would benefit and she would be recognized as an expert.

"Schools should ask local business and sports figures to talk to the kids about their experiences in elementary school. Such revelations enhance the prestige of elementary teachers and give them greater importance in the eyes of their pupils.

"Many industries spend a lot of money developing athletic facilities for its employees' after-hours use. Schools already have these facilities. A physical workout after school to limber tired muscles will go a great way toward eliminating mental weariness.

"Finally, we—teachers, parents, the business community—must work toward raising the status of the teacher in the professional field. The public must perceive teachers as professionals as it did years ago. The health of our educational system depends on the effectiveness and mental attitudes of its teachers. We'll have fewer burned-out teachers when they begin to feel and assume their great influence and importance in the future of the nation."

BURNOUT SURVIVAL KIT FOR THE ROAD

The following may add aid and comfort to you while you battle away the burnout blues.

The Andover Review (Fall 1977) "Teachers on Teaching."

Child Care Quarterly (Summer 1977), Vol. 6, No. 2 "Symposium: Stress and Burn-Out in Child Care."

On Teaching, by Herbert Kohl (Schocken).

Professional Burn-out: A Personal Survival Kit for How to Help Others Without Burning Yourself Out, LeRoy Spaniol, Ph.D. and Jennifer Caputo, Human Services Associates, Massachusetts Ave., Lexington, MA 02173 ($10).

Troubled Teacher, by Esther P. Rothman (McKay).

Contributors: *Andrew J. DuBrin* is psychologist and professor of behavioral sciences, College of Business, Rochester Institute of Technology in New York. *Jerry Fowler* is with Floating Faculty in Prince George's County Schools, Upper Marlboro, Maryland. *Larry Hoiberg* is principal of J. Nelson Kelly School, Grand Forks, North Dakota. *James E. Mathiott* is principal of Ohlone Elementary School, Palo Alto, California. *Faye Morrison* is reading consultant for Palo Alto School District, California. *Peggie Case Paulus* is a sixth-grade English teacher at St. John School, Houston, Texas. *Elizabeth Prince* was a teacher advocate in New Orleans, Louisiana. *Sandy Stein* was a speech and language therapist with the Madison Public Schools, Wisconsin. *Bettie Burres Youngs* is a reading resource teacher for the Des Moines Public Schools in Iowa and the "1976 Iowa Teacher of the Year."

THE NIBBLE METHOD OF OVERCOMING STRESS

Lynn Caine

The first step is to analyze just what is causing your overload. I have found that making a list, getting it all down on paper, is an effective way to start. Write down everything that you dislike about your life and everything that has changed in your life in the last twelve months. That may not cover every stress, but it should come close. A woman's list might read like this:

1. My daughter broke her arm.
2. The people upstairs play their stereo too loud.
3. I just got fired.
4. I can't balance my checkbook.
5. The car needs two new tires, but I don't have the money.
6. My new shoes are killing me.
7. I am overweight, and I hate myself for it.
8. My mother is seriously ill.
9. I've been having spotting between my periods.
10. My ex-husband is three months behind on his child-support payments.

Whatever it is that is making your life a burden, write it down. Then study your list. What can you eliminate? If you were the woman whose miseries are listed above, how would you lighten your stress load?

First of all, your daughter's arm will heal. There is the doctor's bill, of course, but if you explain your circumstances to him—especially numbers three and ten—he will probably let the bill ride for a couple of months. Or you might suggest he send the bill to your ex-husband.

As for problem number two, have you discussed the decibel level with your neighbors? They may be absolutely unaware of your distress. Suggest a compromise. No blasting music after ten in the evening. Or write a funny note. If all else fails, complain to the landlord.

Getting fired is always a shock. But you will get another job, and it may well be better suited to your abilities and talents. For the time being, this is a real stress breeder. The best way to deal with it is to cut down on other stresses so that you can put all your energies into the job hunt.

As for the checkbook, if you really can't balance it, trot on down to the bank. They will help you. And on number five, unless the rubber is worn through, you might just make a point of using the car as little as possible and driving slowly until you get a new job. If the tires are dangerous, and you need the car every day, well, you'd better go ahead and buy new tires. It's better to take on some installment payments than to risk your life—and those of others. If your new shoes are killing you, take them off.

Stop hating yourself for being overweight. Set a date for going on a diet and getting more exercise, like two weeks from today. A month from today. And then stop thinking about your weight until then. When the diet date comes around, your life may be a bit less stressful, and dieting will be easier.

Your mother's illness is worrying you, but if you have done everything you can for her you should not waste energy in useless worry. But you *should* take care of yourself. See the doctor about that spotting between periods. It may be nothing at all, and then you can stop worrying about it. If it is something, then you can take steps to correct it. As for not being able to afford a visit to the doctor, tell him about problems three and ten again. You'll be able to work something out.

And finally, send your ex-husband a letter saying that if his check is not received within the next ten days, he will be hearing from your lawyer.

These may sound like glib solutions, but I do not mean them to be. No one's life is all that simple. But these can serve as guidelines to help you think about lightening the stresses in your own life. Once you start thinking about the problems you have written down, you will find that most of them have at least partial solutions.

But how do you get started at fixing up your life and removing the stresses? First be aware that starting is painful, extremely painful, despite all the Band-Aid therapies that promise so much. To achieve anything worthwhile and lasting, one must prepare for a lot of hard work and self-discipline. Beware of easy answers.

Change is hard and slow and can only be achieved by consistent work. I have had some success with what I call the nibble method, the small steps that build self-confidence. We commit self-sabotage by establishing unrealistic goals for ourselves; instead make goals realistic. If you want to firm up your body don't begin by promising yourself that you will do a hundred sit-ups the first day. Anyone who isn't crippled can do ten revolutions on a stationary bicycle, or two leg raises. Remember that the consistent repetition will become part of you. If you nibble away at your faults, change will come naturally, easily, inevitably.

And one should always be on the lookout for support systems. After Martin died, it took me a long time to realize that it requires generosity to accept generosity. I often refused help, feeling that accepting help would reveal my neediness and incompetence. I felt that unless I could reciprocate, I couldn't accept favors. That was long before I realized that eventually we all need help. Everyone has her turn.

Some years ago, I was working late—too late—because I was struggling over a letter I had to write to a difficult,demanding author. It's not easy to communicate with someone you dislike, and I was unable to find the words. In order to avoid my unpleasant chore, I left my office to see my friend Paula, who was also working late.

Like me, she was also struggling. This intelligent, articulate woman was unable to compose a cablegram she had to send that night to someone she disliked. Whimsically, I suggested that we exchange tasks. I had no mental block about her chore, she had none about mine. We quickly got our work done and went out for an exceptionally pleasant dinner, relieved of our anxiety and resentment.

That incident was the genesis of a support group we formed many years later, the purpose of which was to relieve our friends of as many irritating little chores as possible by exchanging mental blocks. We began by making a list of the tasks we did well and quickly and another list of the things we simply couldn't do.

Peggy is terrific at filling out forms and wrapping packages. Carol excels at almost everything but cannot fill out certain forms and is terrified of making dentist's appointments. Grace, who is a genius at organizing files and anything else, is such a hypochondriac that she is unable to make any kind of doctor's appointment. Cathy is a wonderful shopper, knows where to find everything at bargain prices, but cannot write prompt condolence letters and thank-you notes. I write prompt condolence letters and thank-you notes but procrastinate about paying bills.

We assigned areas of responsibility. Peggy sent for and filled out Carol's forms; I called her children's dentist and made appointments. Carol in turn paid my bills and balanced my checkbook. I called Grace's numerous doctors and made appointments for her—and so forth. Exchanging chores doesn't solve all our problems, but it helps to reduce the stress level for all of us. Besides, it's lots of fun.

Remember, too, that you have options. There is always more than one way to handle any situation. Make a list of your options. After considering them, you may decide that you have already taken the most effective option, or you may hit on something better. Studying your list will also help you realize that time will take care of many of your present sources of stress and that they will disappear eventually. There is nothing one can do to soften the immediate trauma of death or divorce, those high-stress events, but it will help if you are aware that the pain will ease in time, that you will not always hurt this much.

Try to slow down a little. Learn to develop perspective. I don't say stop worrying. Worrying has its constructive side. Someone has described worry as "compulsive pagan prayer," an unconscious plea for help with problems too complicated to solve, burdens too heavy to shoulder.

A recent study at the Medical Institute of Benares Hindu University in India established that Yoga and meditation significantly lower stress. Yoga is not the only way of relieving stress, of course. Almost any kind of strenuous exercise reduces stress—brisk walking, swimming, dancing, bicycling, jogging, jumping rope. Sing a song; it doesn't matter if it's off key, you will feel better for it. Laugh. There is a reason for the telephone company's success with its dial-a-joke service. Laughter cuts stress build-up.

If your stress . . . is too much, . . . depression sets in or psychosomatic ills start plaguing you. [Then] I would advise [you] to reach out for help. Help does not necessarily mean a psychologist. But you should talk to someone. Your doctor may be able to suggest ways to ease your tension, or your minister, priest, rabbi, or other religious counselor may be helpful. Some [people] are blessed with good and wise friends who know how to listen. And often that is all that is needed—a listening ear. As we talk about our problems, they somehow seem to become less terrifying, easier to cope with.

But if you feel that you need professional help, reach out for that, too. Don't feel yourself a failure or incompetent in any way. Seeking help shows that you are intelligent and that you value yourself—a healthy attitude. Finding a good psychologist or therapist is not so difficult as it used to be (except in rural communities). In most areas, your doctor, the hospital, the medical society can refer you to good people.

TWENTY WAYS I SAVE TIME

Alan Lakein

1. I don't waste time regretting my failures.
2. I don't waste my time feeling guilty about what I don't do.
3. I don't read newspapers or magazines (except occasionally).
4. I don't own a television set.
5. I've given up forever all "waiting time." If I have to "wait" I consider it a "gift of time" to relax, plan or do something I would not otherwise have done.
6. I carry blank 3 x 5 index cards in my pocket to jot down notes and ideas.
7. I always plan first thing in the morning and set priorities for the day.
8. I keep a list of specific items to be done each day, arrange them in priority order, and then do my best to get the important ones done as soon as possible.
9. I ask myself, "Would anything terrible happen if I didn't do this priority item?" If the answer is NO, I don't do it.
10. I always use the 80/20 rule. (80 percent of the value comes from doing 20 percent of the items.)
11. I concentrate on one thing at a time.
12. I delegate everything I possibly can to others.
13. I generate as little paperwork as possible and throw away anything I possibly can.
14. I handle each piece of paper only once.
15. I keep my desk top cleared for action and put the most important thing in the center of my desk
16. I have a place for everything (so I waste as little time as possible looking for things).
17. I save up all trivia for a three-hour session once a month.
18. I try not to think of work on the weekends.
19. I relax and "do nothing" rather frequently.
20. I recognize that inevitably some of my time will be spent on activities outside my control and don't fret about it.

HOW TO BRING FORTH THE RELAXATION RESPONSE

Herbert Benson

The case for the use of the Relaxation Response by healthy but harassed individuals is straightforward. It can act as a built-in method of counteracting the stresses of everyday living which bring forth the fight-or-flight response. We have also shown how the Relaxation Response may be used as a new approach to aid in the treatment and perhaps prevention of diseases such as hypertension. In this [article], we will review the components necessary to evoke the Relaxation Response and present a specific technique that we have developed at Harvard's Thorndike Memorial Laboratory and Boston's Beth Israel Hospital. We again emphasize that, for those who may suffer from any disease state, the potential therapeutic use of the Relaxation Response should be practiced only under the care and supervision of a physician.

We reviewed the Eastern and Western religious, cultic, and lay practices that led to the Relaxation Response. From those age-old techniques we have extracted four basic components necessary to bring forth that response:

(1) *A Quiet Environment*

Ideally, you should chose a quiet, calm environment with as few distractions as possible. A quiet room is suitable, as is a place of worship. The quiet environment contributes to the effectiveness of the repeated word or phrase by making it easier to eliminate distracting thoughts.

(2) *A Mental Device*

To shift the mind from logical, externally oriented thought, there should be a constant stimulus: a sound, word, or phrase repeated silently or aloud; or fixed gazing at an object. Since one of the major difficulties in the elicitation of the Relaxation Response is "mind wandering," the repetition of the word or phrase is a way to help break the train of distracting thoughts. Your eyes are usually closed if you are using a repeated sound or word; of course, your eyes are open if you are gazing. Attention to the normal rhythm of breathing is also useful and enhances the repetition of the sound or the word.

(3) *A Passive Attitude*

When distracting thoughts occur, they are to be disregarded and attention redirected to the repetition or gazing; *you should not worry about how well you are performing the technique,* because this may well prevent the Relaxation Response from occurring. Adopt a "let it happen" attitude. *The passive attitude is perhaps the most important element in eliciting the Relaxation Response. Distracting thoughts will occur. Do not worry about them. When these thoughts do present themselves and you become aware of them, simply return to the repetition of the mental device. These other thoughts do not mean you are performing the technique incorrectly. They are to be expected.*

(4) *A Comfortable Position*

A comfortable posture is important so that there is no undue muscular tension. Some methods call for a sitting position. A few practitioners use the cross-legged "lotus" position of the Yogi. If you are lying down, there is a tendency to fall asleep. As we have noted previously, the various postures of kneeling, swaying, or sitting in a cross-legged position are believed to have evolved to prevent falling asleep. You should be comfortable and relaxed.

It is important to remember that there is not a single method that is unique in eliciting the Relaxation Response. For example, Transcendental Meditation is one of the many techniques that incorporate these components. However, we believe it is not necessary to use the specific method and specific *secret*, personal sound taught by Transcendental Meditation. *Tests at the Thorndike Memorial Laboratory of Harvard have shown that a similar technique used with any sound or phrase or prayer or mantra brings forth the same physiologic changes noted during Transcendental Meditation:* decreased oxygen consumption; decreased carbon-dioxide elimination; decreased rate of breathing. In other words using the basic necessary components, any one of the age-old or the newly derived techniques produces the same physiologic results regardless of the mental device used. The following set of instructions, used to elicit the Relaxation

Response, was developed by our group at Harvard's Thorndike Memorial Laboratory and was found to produce the same physiologic changes we had observed during the practice of Transcendental Meditation. This technique is now being used to lower blood pressure in certain patients. A noncultic technique, it is drawn with little embellishment from the four basic components found in the myriad of historical methods. We claim no innovation but simply a scientific validation of age-old wisdom. The technique is our current method of eliciting the Relaxation Response in our continuing studies at the Beth Israel Hospital of Boston.

(1) *Sit quietly in a comfortable position.*

(2) *Close your eyes.*

(3) *Deeply relax all your muscles, beginning at your feet and progressing up to your face. Keep them relaxed.*

(4) *Breathe through your nose. Become aware of your breathing. As you breathe out, say the word, "ONE," silently to yourself. For example, breathe IN . . . OUT, "ONE"; IN . . . OUT, "ONE"; etc. Breathe easily and naturally.*

(5) *Continue for 10 to 20 minutes. You may open your eyes to check the time, but do not use an alarm. When you finish, sit quietly for several minutes, at first with your eyes closed and later with your eyes opened. Do not stand up for a few minutes.*

(6) *Do not worry about whether you are successful in achieving a deep level of relaxation. Maintain a passive attitude and permit relaxation to occur at its own pace. When distracting thoughts occur, try to ignore them by not dwelling upon them and return to repeating "ONE." With practice, the response should come with little effort. Practice the technique once or twice daily, but not within two hours after any meal, since the digestive processes seem to interfere with the elicitation of the Relaxation Response.*

The subjective feelings that accompany the elicitation of the Relaxation response vary among individuals. The majority of people feel a sense of calm and feel very relaxed. A small percentage of people immediately experience ecstatic feelings. Other descriptions that have been related to us involve feelings of pleasure, refreshment, and well-being. Still others have noted relatively little change on a subjective level. Regardless of the subjective feelings described by our subjects, we have found that the physiologic changes such as decreased oxygen consumption are taking place.

There is no educational requirement or aptitude necessary to experience the Relaxation Response. Just as each of us experiences anger, contentment, and excitment, each has the capacity to experience the Relaxation Response. It is an innate response within us. Again, there are many ways in which people bring forth the Relaxation Response, and your own individual considerations may be applied to the four components involved. You may wish to use the technique we have presented but with a different mental device. You may use a syllable or phrase that may be easily repeated and sounds natural to you.

Another technique you may wish to use is a prayer from your religious tradition. Choose a prayer that incorporates the four elements necessary to bring forth the Relaxation Response. As we have shown . . . we believe every religion has such prayers. We would reemphasize that we do not view religion in a mechanistic fashion simply because a religious prayer brings forth this desired physiologic response. Rather, we believe, as did William James, that these age-old prayers are one way to remedy an inner incompleteness and to reduce inner discord. Obviously, there are many other aspects to religious beliefs and practices which have little to do with the Relaxation Response. However, there is little reason not to make use of an appropriate prayer within the framework of your own beliefs if you are most comfortable with it.

Your individual considerations of a particular technique may place different emphasis upon the components necessary to elicit the Relaxation Response and also may incorporate various practices into the use of the technique. For example, for some a quiet environment with little distraction is crucial. However, others prefer to practice the Relaxation Response in subways or trains. Some people choose always to practice the Relaxation Response in the same place at a regular time.

Since the daily use of the Relaxation Response necessitates a slight change in life-style, some find it difficult at first to keep track of the regularity with which they evoke the Response. In our investigations of the Relaxation Response, patients use [a] calendar. . . . Each time they practice the Relaxation Response, they make a check in the appropriate [place].

It may be said, as an aside, that many people have told us that they use our technique for evoking the Relaxation Response while lying in bed to help them fall asleep. Some have even given up sleeping pills as a result. It should be noted, however, that when you fall asleep using the technique, you are not experiencing the Relaxation Response, you are asleep. As we have shown, the Relaxation Response is different from sleep. . . .

One should not use the Relaxation Response in an effort to shield oneself or to withdraw from the pressures of the outside world which are necessary for everyday functioning. *The fight-or-flight response is often appropriate and should not be thought of as always harmful. It is a necessary part of our physiologic and psychological makeup, a useful reaction to many situations in our current world.* Modern society has forced us to evoke the fight-or-flight response repeatedly. We are not using it as we believe our ancestors used it. That is, we do not always run, nor do we fight when it is elicited. However, our body is being prepared for running or for fighting, and since this preparation is not always utilized, we believe anxieties, hypertension and its related diseases ensue. The Relaxation Response offers a natural balance to counteract the undesirable manifestations of the fight-or-flight response. We do not believe that you will become a passive and withdrawn person and less able to function and compete in our world because you regularly elicit the Relaxation Response. Rather, it has been our experience that people who regularly evoke the Relaxation Response claim they are more effective in dealing with situations that probably bring forth the fight-or-flight response. We believe you will be able to cope better with difficult situations by regularly allowing your body to achieve a more balanced state through the physiologic effects of the Relaxation Response. You can expect this balanced state to last as long as you regularly bring forth the response. Within several days after stopping its regular use, we believe, you will cease to benefit from its effects, *regardless* of the technique employed, be it prayer, Transcendental Meditation or the method proposed in this book.

HOW TO DRAW VITALITY FROM STRESS

Rosalind Forbes

Stress seekers rank high in intelligence, emotional stability, ambition and leadership, according to psychologist Bruce Ogilvie, Ph.D., of San Jose State University. With so much going for them already, what stress gives them is a competitive edge.

The adrenaline shooting through the body of a stress seeker produces a euphoria equal to that of an addictive drug. The addiction is strongest in skilled athletes whose triumphs and defeats are shared by enthusiastic crowds.

No wonder they maintain a positive attitude toward reasonable amounts of stress. Their secret for handling it constructively and using it to advantage is not to let it get beyond manageable limits. Were it to exceed those limits, stress seekers would be in danger of becoming stress victims.

Too much stress limits performance; too little stress takes away motivation. Stress seekers have learned to gauge stress for the activity at hand. At times, they may find ways to "gear up."

STRESS MEANS ENERGY TO SOME

In their own way, stress seekers have learned to direct their energies toward the job that needs to be done. The athlete would say he is trying to be "on edge during competition." The business person would say he is "in top form." In their reactions to stress or anticipated stress, they are both striving for the same thing: to be at optimal stress levels for the task at hand. "The kind of stress I feel before a race is a nervousness, a feeling of energy," claimed gold-medal marathon-runner Frank Shorter. "I feel hyper and very excited, and I try to channel this energy into the competitive event and use it to my advantage."

Although they are probably most easily found in the athletic, business, and entertainment worlds, stress seekers occur in all walks of life. They are not afraid to take risks, to question or change traditional life-styles if

---

they don't fit, to choose what is right for them. With tremendous odds against them, instead of giving up, most stress seekers will be even more strongly motivated by the challenge.

CREATIVE WORK AND RISK ARE ESSENTIAL TO STRESS SEEKERS

Marvin Zuckerman, Ph.D., program director of clinical psychology at the University of Delaware, talks of four expressions of stress seeking. One of these is the desire to seek excitement in socially acceptable but risky activities such as skydiving or racing cars.

A second expression of stress seeking involves the desire to seek sensation through the mind and senses and nonconforming life-styles. Stress seekers usually chafe if they are forced to live conventional middle-class lives.

They best express themselves through creative work, frequent travel, novel friends and unstructured living. Dr. Zuckerman refers to the stress seeker's need for people as sources of stimulation as "disinhibition," the third kind of expression.

A final mode of expressing stress seeking has to do with "boredom susceptibility." Stress seekers have a low tolerance for repetitious activities. They become discontented and restless if they go for long periods of time without outside stimulation.

This is not to say stress seekers cannot live middle-class existences or hold eight-hour-a-day jobs. Some simply find their outlets through high-risk avocational activities, like parachute jumping.

Dr. Zuckerman suggests there may be a biological need for high stimulation in some people. "High-sensation seekers have a stronger physiological response to novel stimuli of moderate intensity, as measured by galvanic skin response, than low-sensation seekers. They may need constant variety in order to reach their own high optimal level of arousal, the level that feels best," or at which they perform most efficiently. The psychologist goes on to say that genetic factors may be responsible for this.

Understandably, social factors cannot be overlooked. Parents who are stress seekers, who enjoy high stimulation, most likely live in high-stimulus environments. Children growing up in these households probably will turn out the same way.

The talent for managing and utilizing stress can be honed or blunted in almost anyone. To test your stress-seeking tendencies, take the test [at the end of this chapter]. If you find you need some improvement, here are some suggestions:

WAYS TO BECOME MORE OF A STRESS SEEKER

1. Turn every obstacle or problem into a creative solution. In learning to overcome problems, you gain confidence in your inner strength, judgment and resources. Remind yourself that you have had both big and small problems to deal with in the past and you have managed to come through them just fine. Have several alternative solutions if things don't go exactly as planned. Most people learn by trial and error.
2. Don't be afraid to make mistakes or even fail. When you make mistakes, correct them and move forward. However, winning should not be your main objective either. You should be motivated by the desire to put forth your best effort and concentrate on the task at hand. Set your own standards of excellence, and work toward achieving those things which are important to you.
3. Get involved in a sport or hobby that is exciting and daring. Try something you never thought you could do. Make it something entirely different from anything you have done before.
4. Set priorities. You will never accomplish everything you would like to, so decide which things are of real value to you and eliminate the others. In the process of elimination, you may remove certain time-consuming or energy-draining people or activities from your life.
5. Form a mental picture of yourself as you would like to be, the potential you. Realize that what you are today is the result of your image and beliefs of what you could be. If you do not like what you see, form a new mental picture with the qualities you want to possess.
6. Evaluate your present work or job. Does your job provide you with just a living, or is it something you enjoy? Try to have a good fit between your abilities and skills and your work.
7. Learn the secret of the professionals, who totally immerse themselves in what they are doing. Focus all your awareness and concentration on the present moment. Forget about the past or the future. This allows you to respond totally and fully to your imediate environment. By keeping actively involved in what you are doing, you're less likely to get bored.
8. Use some guided fantasy to come down physically or mentally after a tension-producing event. Imagine yourself floating on a rubber raft in a calm, still lake with the sun on your body and a cool drink in your hand. Imagine yourself at this point feeling so comfortable and so relaxed that you can't move a single muscle in your body. When you feel ready to return to reality, begin counting backward from five to one, coming back to the facts of your situation slowly.

9. Don't allow criticism to stop you. Remember no one is perfect, least of all your critic.
10. What are you doing today to improve yourself? There is a certain principle which says that if we do not move forward we stagnate. Each time you do something to develop yourself, you contribute to your feelings of self-worth and learn to respect your uniqueness.

Find Your Own Comfortable Stress Level

To a degree, it is to everyone's advantage to seek stress. The key to successful usage of it is to seek the right types of stress and then learn how to concentrate on only one thing at a time so that the stress does not become overwhelming.

All of us have an optimum level of stress under which we reach our own most productive peak. This level varies from individual to individual, so it is important to determine where that level is for you. Once you decide what your optimum stress level is, you have the key to learning how to function at the height of your productivity.

ARE YOU A STRESS SEEKER?

Take this test to determine the role you let stress play in your life. Rate yourself as to how you typically react in each of the situations listed: 4—Always, 3—Frequently, 2—Sometimes, 1—Never.

______ 1. Do you have a tendency to put things off until the last minute and then frantically rush to get them done?

______ 2. Do you thrive on situations in which there is pressure, competition, tension, or risk?

______ 3. Do you find stress or tension has been a driving force behind many of your major accomplishments?

______ 4. Do you feel exhilarated or energized after accomplishing a difficult task or closing an important business deal?

______ 5. Do you enjoy novelty and challege in your work?

______ 6. Do you have a tendency to see obstacles as challenges rather than headaches?

______ 7. Are you constantly seeking ways to improve yourself or your performance in your field?

______ 8. In general, would you classify yourself as a risk taker rather than a risk avoider?

______ 9. Are you willing to give up job security for job challenge?

______10. Are you able to "come down" physically and emotionally a few hours after a tension-producing event?

______11. Do you seek action-oriented vacations?

______12. In your leisure time do you pursue activities in which there is a certain amount of danger or risk? (Examples: skydiving, rock climbing.)

Answer Key

If your score is between 36 and 48, you are a true stress seeker who enjoys excitement and exhilaration.

If your score is between 24 and 35, you probably like to balance challenge with risks so that you stay on an even keel.

A score between 12 and 23 indicates that you are likely to avoid stress and seek security instead.

SIX STEPS TO A POSITIVE ADDICTION

William Glasser

While I was having a discussion on positive addiction with a group of educators in May 1974, a woman of about thirty-five stood up and said that she was addicted to bicycle riding. She explained that every evening after supper, usually between six and seven, she rode her bicycle for an hour by herself around her neighborhood. Having not yet arrived at the concept of the PA state, I was mostly concerned with the discomfort she felt if she didn't ride her bike, so I asked her, "What happens if you don't ride your bike?" She replied, "Nothing happens, because I always ride my bike." Her statement was so definite that I asked her in a teasing way, "Well, what if one of your children were very sick and needed care, wouldn't you skip your bike ride?" Her half-humorous, half-serious reply was, "They better not get sick during the hour after dinner that I ride my bike." She stated something that I have since heard from almost everyone who has a positive addiction: the time they have set aside for whatever they do that they are addicted to is sacrosanct. They want neither the pain nor the loss of pleasure that accompanies skipping their habit. . . .

A positive addiction can be anything at all that a person chooses to do as long as it fulfills the following six criteria: (1) It is something noncompetitive that you choose to do and you can devote an hour (approximately) a day to it. (2) It is possible for you to do it easily and it doesn't take a great deal of mental effort to do it well. (3) You can do it alone or rarely with others but it does not depend upon others to do it. (4) You believe that it has some value (physical, mental, or spiritual) for you. (5) You believe that if you persist at it you will improve, but this is completely subjective—you need to be the only one who measures that improvement. (6) The activity *must* have the quality that you can do it *without criticizing yourself. If you can't accept yourself during this time the activity will not be addicting*. This is why it is so important that the activity can be done alone. Any time you introduce other people you chance introducing competition or criticism, often both. Risking

---

criticism can be detrimental to the PA state, which is why many positive addicts keep quiet about what they do. . . . This point . . . was perhaps best stated by one woman who discovered a form of meditation on her own:

> For a long time I did not discuss it [meditation] with anyone because I feared it was some kind of psychotic experience, mental disorder . . . or if not, at least it would certainly sound like it to another. I no longer feel this way. I live a productive and good life and wonder why everyone doesn't use this gift which I am convinced all have access to but few ever use.

Even if you follow all of the six criteria for positive addiction there is absolutely no guarantee that you will succeed in becoming addicted. To become addicted you have to reach the PA state on a regular basis at least several times a week for several minutes to an hour each time.. If this happens, then you experience a surge of pleasure which you learn to crave. If you deny yourself the PA activity for as little as three or four days you will suffer fairly severe withdrawal pain both physical and mental. . . . Many meditators as well as many others who fulfill the six criteria do gain strength from their practice but they don't reach addiction. If they continue they may eventually become addicted and gain much more strength, but most meditators are not positive addicts. They may experience brief flashes of the PA state but not enough so they suffer any significant withdrawal. Mostly what they achieve is a pleasant, relaxing habit which many of the respondents have erroneously reported as addiction. Although it doesn't happen often, it is possible to become addicted to any physical or mental activity by fulfilling the six criteria. I would like to describe some of the practices that people have reported as positive addictions, again with the caution that just because they are reported as PA does not make them so. My estimate is that of all the reported positive addictions, running, yoga, and meditating are the only practices in which people reach PA in significant numbers.

There are, therefore, two major categories of PA—the physical, led by the runners, and the mental, dominated by the meditators (yoga can be part physical and part mental). . . . Under the mental practices, people have responded that they daydream and have also mentioned that it was a relief to have this practice verified as beneficial. As adults they have had difficulty admitting to this practice because daydreaming is something that you are supposed to do only as a small child and, unfortunately, even then not too much. Closely allied to meditating and daydreaming are a large group of routine, nontaxing physical activities, which I classify as mental because they can be done for long periods with almost no effort or conscious concentration.

Examples of these are knitting, crocheting, needlepoint, tatting. Another group responds that gardening is their PA. One woman says, "Every day I mess around with houseplants and suffer if I skip a day." Quite a few people report that their PA is writing in a personal journal. Creative writing might possibly be addicting for great writers like Hemingway, who wrote regularly each morning from six to ten, but it is too self-critical an activity to be addicting to the nonprofessional. On the other hand, keeping a journal is a highly non-self-critical activity (if it weren't no one could endure the pain) and those who do it say that their minds frequently spin off as they record their day's activities, thoughts, and feelings. One woman says she is addicted to taking baths, three baths a day in which she sits and drifts in the warm water, not washing, just soaking up the aloneness of her warm, pleasant, self-taught meditatory experience. She too was grateful that the PA concept helped her to understand a habit she knew was good but was hesitant to talk about. One woman says that she is addicted to grooming herself and to applying makeup, has been doing it for ten years for forty-five minutes a day, and says she became addicted two months after she started. When she skips a day she feel unattractive and insecure, less capable of handling unusual situations. With it she has much more confidence.

Other people play musical instruments—the piano, the flute, the guitar, and the banjo are commonly mentioned—some sing, and many listen to music. These are all regarded by people as positively addicting. Practicing an instrument is perhaps more so for most than listening because it occupies one more and also provides more of a sense of accomplishment, but I suppose if one can become an addicted warm-bath taker, one can be an addicted listener. Although I have had no such responses, I would also venture that composing music must be for many a PA practice. Beethoven couldn't even hear his music much of his life but he heard it in his brain, and composing must to some extent have been a positive addiction that kept him going after he lost his hearing. Again, a word of caution. While any of these or similar activities can be pursued to addiction, it is my belief that this is extremely rare.

Yoga is both a physical and a mental discipline, and many people who practice yoga eventually reach PA. One women reports that she stands in the bow position and vibrates in other positions taught to her in what she calls bioenergetics, which seems to be a type of yoga. Quite a few practice Hatha Yoga, which involves special physical exercises or asanas. Others stress yogic breathing or relaxation. But all these people are engaged in a rigorous physical and mental discipline which is either yoga or very close to it, whatever it may be called.

From here we go to the large group of physical addictions headed by running, but which also includes hiking, exercising, weight lifting, swimming, bicycling, and perhaps rock climbing or mountain climbing. Although rock climbing and mountain climbing are not something a person usually can do on a daily basis, I am sure the PA state which climbers occasionally reach in their activities is what motivates them. I don't believe that these can be classified in the same way as exercising or running but maybe they are to PA as a binge is to negative addiction. While running is the most common of all the physical positive addiction, ... there are probably many more physical addictions than I have listed here. I make no claim to have discovered them all. Again, I stress that if an activity fulfills the six criteria stated earlier in this chapter it is potentially addicting. A friend of mine recently suggested that I should investigate bird watching as a potential PA activity. Considering the number of fanatic bird watchers, who is to say it's not?

... A man addicted to singing, who has been doing it for at least an hour a day for four years, says when he doesn't sing: "I feel lousy inside, lazy, like I haven't completed something. I am definitely a better musician but also a more confident person." Person after person describes the discomfort as feeling grumpy, hard to get along with, upset with himself or herself. Some say their day doesn't go right, and in most cases they say they feel guilt because they have missed something important that they didn't have to miss. In fact, many people just write the word "guilty" and that sums it up. Some people say they feel more tension, more nervousness, more self-doubt; others that they are more impatient, less communicative with others, and irritable. Several people describe fatigue, a feeling of tiredness or deadness, if they don't do their addicting thing. One person describes, "My mind feels a little muddled or foggy." All of these descriptions occur over and over again on the positive addiction form but they occur more in the physical addictions than in the mental practices.

Then we come to the question "What benefits do you receive from your addiction?" People, especially in the physical addictions or yoga, describe weight loss or an ability to control their weight where it was out of control before. Many say they have been able to give up bad habits, quite often excess drinking, sometimes smoking. People describe mental alertess, increased self-awareness, a physical feeling of well-being. Over and over again people report a *sense of confidence*, perhaps the single most often used words to describe the benefits of their addiction. Many describe that they are more tolerant and less angry. All of these are obviously tied to increased mental strength.... All of the people who engage in the physical addictions—

running, exercising—describe themselves in better physical shape naturally, but many of the people who engage in a purely mental addiction like meditation also describe physical benefits, especially an ability to control overweight. Both physical and mental positive addicts say they have more energy and need less sleep.

. . . What is important here is to realize that PA is available to anyone. It has no age limits or activity limits. It can be attempted by the aged and the infirm, as well as by the young and the healthy. The only condition is that to get its benefits you have to do it usually for several months, sometimes for years.

Where you get the strength to do it long enough to gain more strength is a question I can't answer. It is like looking for your first job and being told only experienced people are hired. It's "Catch 22" except that people do get hired and people, even some weak people, do have the strength to become positively addicted. I believe that in the beginning the person is helped to continue by experiencing the non-self-critical state, which is pleasant and relaxing but not addicting. Later he may experience flashes of the PA state that further help to keep him going. While all positive addicts must do something they want to do, what is most important, I believe, is to figure out how to do whatever it is that you choose in such a way that you can accept yourself completely and noncritically as you do it. If you can't do this, then you have little chance to become addicted. So, if you choose, choose carefully. Don't expect too much of yourself and don't make a big deal about the fact that you are attempting to become addicted. Go quietly. It's a personal thing. Keep it that way and you have a good chance to reach PA.

POSITIVE DENIAL: THE CASE FOR NOT FACING REALITY

Richard Lazarus
(Interviewed by Daniel Goleman)

Goleman: How do you define stress?

Lazarus: Psychological stress resides neither in the situation nor in the person; it depends on a transaction between the two. It arises from how the person appraises an event and adapts to it. Stress is what occurs when the demands of the environment, in the person's eyes, clearly exceed the resources of the person to handle them. Foremost among those resources is how the person construes the situation: does he or she judge it as threatening, or as a challenge? . . . [At that moment Lazarus' phone rings.]

Goleman: There's one of life's hassles.

Lazarus: This interruption isn't very stressful. It doesn't have great significance for either of us. It's a minor nuisance. But that's precisely the point. How you relate to these things makes all the difference.

I think of the lines from Charles Bukowski's poem "The Shoelace": "It's not the large things that/send a man to the/madhouse. . . . / not the death of his love / but a shoelace that snaps / with no time left. . . ."

When people get upset over what seem to be trivialities, it's because the trivial symbolizes for them something of tremendous import. When the shoelace breaks, the psychological stress is from the implication that you cannot control your own life, that you're helpless in the face of the most stupid trivialities—or, even worse, that such things happen because of your own inadequacies in the first place. . . .

Goleman: Why do you say you see some value in self-deception?

Lazarus: . . . . Researchers studying victims of severe burns and of paralysis from polio . . . found that self-deception, through denial of the

---

severity of incapacitating disease, was a valuable first step in coping. At the beginning, when the victims are confused and weak, it's hardest then for them to act realistically. In severe crisis, denial buys preparation time; it lets the person face the grim facts at a gradual, manageable pace. Robert Jay Lifton and Elisabeth Kubler-Ross have found the same thing in those facing death. In all these instances, a temporary disavowal of reality helps the person get through the devastating early period of loss and threat. Later they can face the facts and mobilize other coping efforts. In short, there are times when ignorance is better than truth.

Goleman: Even so, a hallmark of psychosis is a break with reality.

Lazarus: The paradox is that both things are true: illusions can be a sign of pathology, or they can make life worth living.

Goleman: Then it's not either/or; it's both/and. The problem is to find the context that makes each true. When do illusions help or hinder?

Lazarus: To answer the question, you first have to differentiate among the types of denial and illusion. Denial and illusion are vague ideas, they include a multitude of ways of thinking.

Goleman: How do denial and illusion differ?

Lazarus: They're closely related. Denial of the facts clears the way for illusion. For example, a person can deny the facts of his illness, but eventually the illusions that denial allows become very difficult to sustain. If it's an illnes that becomes progressively worse, the evidence is harder and harder to overlook. To do so resembles a psychotic denial, a disavowal of reality. Such extreme cases of denial can be dangerous, like the man who ran up the stairs to convince himself he wasn't having a heart attack.

Goleman: One kind of pathological denial, then, is to deceive yourself about medical facts—at your own risk.

Lazarus: That sort of denial is damaging, but in other circumstances it may not be. Illusion can sometimes allow hope, which is healthy. The critical determinant is whether you're denying facts or implications. Implications are ambiguous. Let's say I get a biopsy that says I have a malignant tumor. I can face facts, decide that this is a terrible illness, that I'm in trouble, will die very soon, and so give up hope. Or I can face the fact that this is a serious illness, but acknowledge the ambiguity: people sometimes recover; it's curable. I've got to be treated, but I don't have to give up.

Life is ambiguous. Many of the beliefs we have about the world around us—about justice, about our integrity, about the attitudes of those around us, about our own future—are based on, at best, ambiguous information. One can maintain illusions about those that have a positive aura without necessarily distorting reality. Such illusions are not pathological; hope is not the same as denial.

Another distinction to make is between avoidance and denial. Take a person with a terminal illness who won't talk about it. That person is not necessarily denying the facts of the illness, but simply avoids talking about it, as a means of self-protection. Constant discussion of an illness can discourage hope, and hope is needed when you recognize that the situation is bad. Hope is not pathological: it's often a good prognostic sign.

You find the same thing with people who discover they have other kinds of severe illnesses, incapacitating ones like polio, spinal-cord injury, stroke. There's a crisis period when the person is in real trouble and engages in something that looks like denial of the severity of the problem. The spinal-cord patient hopes he can recover, although the reality is that in most cases, very little return of lost function is likely.

A denial at the outset is functional. For example, rehabilitation in spinal-cord injury depends on the person's struggling to move. Denial keeps the patient's morale up when he or she is most vulnerable. Only later does the patient need to assimilate the reality of the situation.

Goleman: How do you find most people handle the garden-variety of stress?

Lazarus: There are two main varieties of coping. One is problem-solving, the other emotion-focused. Problem-solving coping refers to efforts to change the troublesome situation for the better. It might be useful, say, when you're going to talk with someone at work who makes you anxious, someone you can't stand but you have to see day after day. That's stress you know is going to happen, so you can spend a little time thinking about how you'll handle it. That sort of preparatory coping is the best way to take care of anticipatory stress. You rehearse, and you solve the problem of how to handle the person in your own mind. This coping strategy is very effective—except that not all stress is something you can do anything about. There are some realities you just can't change.

Emotion-focused modes include things you do or say to yourself to feel better which do not alter the actual relationship between a person and the environment. They include many varieties, prominent among which are denial, minimizing, distancing yourself, paying no attention, taking a tranquilizer, thinking of something else, and joking or making light of a situation. They could also be called intra-psychic or cognitive modes of coping, in contrast to efforts to change things.

An enormous amount of coping is emotion-focused. One mistake that's been made in thinking about stress is to believe that healthy people use problem-focused modes, and sick people use emotion-focused ones. For many serious sources of stress in life, there's little or nothing that can be done to change things. If so, you're better off if you do nothing except take care of your feelings.

Goleman: Why raise your blood pressure over something you can't change?

Lazarus: Precisely. That remedy is worse than the disease. We found that in almost every stressful encounter, well-functioning people use a mixture of problem-focused and emotion-focused coping. . . .

Goleman: It seems to me that, at least in theory, the competent coper would be the one who is flexible, uses vigilance when problem-solving is called for and denial when there's nothing to be done, and so on. The person who is stuck in one mode only would be the one in trouble.

Lazarus: That's a reasonable hunch. The people who get into psychological trouble under stress probably approach coping in a rigid way. They use the same strategy, whether or not it's productive.

Goleman: But isn't there a paradox here? On the one hand, effective coping with stress demands flexible tuning of response; on the other, stress itself makes a person less flexible.

Lazarus: Here's where the difference between a threat and a challenge counts. Threat is a state in which the person feels oppressed, blocked, reduced. Coping is poor. But challenge actually facilitates functioning. When a person is challenged, he's more apt to be loose, to use skills effectively.

You find out you're being laid off. Are you losing a job, or getting a chance for a new start? Life is full of events we can see in either light. But this sort of positive reappraisal is just one of many possibilities for cognitive coping.

Goleman: Can we become better stress copers?

Lazarus: [To some extent.] The notion of the competent coper implies that there is some set of resources that a person has that will get him through everything—hassles on the job, death of a spouse, a promotion, illness, moving. But competent people have their troubles. They get into difficulties they can't quite handle. The concept of competence does not imply that a person who is skilled, able, and flexible will always be able to master every situation or handle every stress effectively. Skills that work superbly in one situation—say, as a supervisor—may render a person inept in others—say in intimate relationships.

It's perfectly possible to find tremendous gaps in a person's ability to cope with stress at one period of his life as compared with another, or in one arena as compared with others. We mustn't get magical in our thinking about flexibility, or suppose we'll find people who are always able to manage optimally. That's an ideal probably no one achieves.

CONQUERING COMMON STRESSORS

Alfred S. Alschuler

Let's assume that you cope well, know how to relax, have a positive addiction, and save as much time as you can. As long as school is a combat zone, you must battle alone and continue indefinitely to heal your wounds. Even if your school is only a mildly stressful place, it is to your advantage and in the interests of students and administrators to reduce the overall level of the stressors. Primary prevention can be accomplished by groups in five steps: (1) listing stressors, (2) categorizing the stressors, (3) prioritizing the stressors, (4) planning a campaign to reduce the stressors, (5) implementing the plan. The first four steps can be accomplished in about an hour with a minimum of five people. Thirty to sixty people can participate and each step can be extended in time as appropriate. This problem-solving process is useful in classrooms to create a collaborative, more orderly, and productive learning climate; in in-service education meetings to focus on improving crucial aspects of the teaching environment; or in families to change persistent conflict situations. Wherever it is used, an important feature of this "stress hunt" is the cooperation it establishes among individuals. The common targets are stressful situations, not stressful individuals.[1]

Step 1. Describe three stressful incidents.

Ask each person to describe at least three real, stressful events that occurred during a recent specific 24-hour period. Descriptions should be in one to three sentences on a slip of paper or on a 3 x 5 card. It should be noted that some stresses affecting teachers' work occur before and after school. A few such incidents are useful in the sample generated by participants. Ten minutes is usually sufficient for this procedure.

Step 2. Categorize the list of stressful incidents.

Have one or two volunteers take the entire set of incidents to a quiet place away from the group and arrange them in six to ten categories. The divisions should emerge, fitting the particular set of incidents from the group, and should communicate clearly to the group. Polysyllabic, latinate Brobdingnagian words from the lexicon of scientific psychology are usually not helpful. The labels of each group will be somewhat different. Several sample lists will provide an idea of the range of possibilities.

The following is a compilation of stressors from several different groups of teachers:

1. Clerical work
2. Interruptions that disrupt class
3. Discipline problems with students
4. Lack of equipment and materials
5. Lack of teacher input in decision making
6. Rigid curriculum
7. Destruction of school property
8. Conflicts with administrators
9. Problems with parents
10. Class size
11. Lack of planning time
12. Problems with other teachers
13. Feelings of powerlessness
14. Problems with racist and sexist attitudes and actions.

Not all of these categories will appear in every group of teachers, and most groups will have several categories unique to their situation.

The following stressors were listed by Santa Barbara (California) junior high school students:[2]

1. Getting up in the morning
2. Going to classes
3. Being bored
4. Hassles with teachers
5. Homework
6. Getting bad grades
7. Taking the bus
8. Having to respond in class
9. Food in the cafeteria
10. Not being prepared
11. Hassles with classmates
12. Being tardy.

In a recent survey of 1,200 Oregon school administrators, Boyd Swent and Walter Gmelch[3] found the following 10 stressful conditions cited most frequently among the 35 situations listed on their questionnaires:

1. Complying with state, federal, and organizational rules and policies
2. Participating in meetings that take up too much time
3. Trying to complete reports and other paperwork on time
4. Trying to gain public approval and/or financial support for school programs
5. Trying to resolve parent/school conflicts
6. Evaluating staff members' performance
7. Having to make decisions that affect the lives of individuals whom I know
8. Feeling that I have too heavy a workload, one that I cannot possibly finish during a normal workday
9. Imposing excessively high expections on myself
10. Being interrupted frequently.

Categorizing the incidents may take 15 to 25 minutes. During this waiting period it is often useful for the group (or subgroups of five, if the group is large) to discuss "High Points in My Day": What went well today? Was there a particularly gratifying or rewarding event?

Step 3. Prioritize the categories.

List the categories publicly on a blackboard or on newsprint, defining, explaining, and illustrating them. When the categories are understood, ask participants to vote for the three which are most important and most distressful. A simple hand count is sufficient. If necessary conduct tie-breaking votes. The explanation and voting can usually be completed in about 10 minutes.

Step 4. Develop a plan to reduce the most important stressor.

An efficient way to develop a plan of action is to start with a brainstorming session for 10 minutes or less. List at least 20 different ideas as possible first steps for reducing the most important stressor. Remember the rules for brainstorming: the more ideas the better; don't worry about quality since refinements can be made later; absolutely no criticizing or debating the ideas; the wilder the ideas the better; build on other people's notions by adding to or expanding on them. After brainstorming, conduct another vote for the three ideas each person would most like to develop and see implemented. After identifying these three possibilities, ask participants to choose one of three working groups whose objective in the next 15 minutes is to answer the question: Who will do what by when? When each working group has reported its decisions and a time for a followup meeting has been determined, the session is completed.

Step 5. Implement the plan.

Reducing the stressors in the environment is sometimes a simple matter. In one school, PA announcements during the middle of class periods were causing an average interruption of four minutes throughout the school. According to the teachers' contract, only the first and last five minutes were to be used for such announcements. A delegation of teachers was therefore chosen to speak with the administrators who readily agreed to confine their announcements.

In one elementary school, the students' most stressful experience was having mashed potatoes thrown on their trays at lunch. A student delegation went to the servers to find out the pressures they were experiencing. The questions from this sympathetic group of fourth graders were enough to increase the gentleness of the servers. In one home, the key stress was noise and the chief culprit: TV. The family sold their TV, had greater quiet, more quality time together, and a little extra cash for Christmas presents.

The foregoing method for conquering common stressors is based on three explicit values: working collaboratively, acting democratically, and changing the environmental stressors rather than attempting to reform individuals. If these values are kept in mind as guidelines during the problem-solving process, not only will good working relationships be ensured, but the relationships will lead to a better working climate.

REFERENCES

[1]More complete descriptions of this process can be found in the NEA tape series *Resolving Classroom Conflict Through Social Literacy*, "Conquering Burnout"; and in *School Discipline* by Alfred S. Alschuler (New York: McGraw-Hill Book Co., 1980), "Conquering Burnout, Battle Fatigue, and Frenzy."

[2]My thanks to Gary Mason and his students for sharing this list.

[3]*Stress at the Desk and How to Cope Creatively*, Oregon School Study Council Bulletin 21, no. 4 (1977).

Part Three: Workshop Guide

WORKSHOP GUIDE FOR REDUCING AND PREVENTING TEACHER BURNOUT

Alfred S. Alschuler

Paradoxically, teacher burnout is, in part, the result of caring—about students, about doing a good job, about achieving the best results for students. For over 20 years, this idealism has occurred in schools while the public has demanded more and more and provided less and less support of all kinds—financing, physical security, instructional materials, and public confidence. Teachers have been the first victims of this receding tide. They are burning out faster and dropping out sooner, taking refuge in other jobs—from becoming graduate students to driving subway trains. This transformation of consciousness from love to hate, from hope to cynicism, from commitment to revulsion is a tragedy for students, for parents, for colleagues, and for loved ones—and ultimately for the national welfare.

How is it possible to reverse this twenty-year trend? At most, this book is a drop—but, it is hoped, the right kind of drop. Fortunately there are ways to spot burnout early, reduce stress, and cope more effectively—many requiring little time and no money. The purpose of this section of *Teacher Burnout* is to describe these methods of prevention and healing.

Because most of the methods are learned more easily with others (some involve partnerships), the techniques are described in the context of teacher-conducted workshops. Many of the activities, however, do not require workshops to be learned. Each session follows the same format:

1. An introduction by the session's facilitator, describing the objectives and previewing the agenda
2. Ten minutes in dyad support groups in which each person has five minutes to express any feelings and to receive verbal or behavioral support from the other person
3. An activity implementing one of the six strategies for preventing or reducing burnout
4. Evaluation of the session in order to assist participants in working together even more effectively during the next session; and planning for the next activity, including decisions about time, place, and session facilitator.

The remainder of this workshop guide is divided into two sections: (1) the activities* for the sessions; and (2) the three roles necessary for these workshops to function effectively: the initiator, the session facilitator, and the workshop participants. It is not important that all the activities be done, in sequence, or as presented here. It is important that some deliberate, potent action be taken to conquer burnout and restore teachers' energy, satisfaction, and loving attitudes.

WORKSHOP ACTIVITIES

The campaign against burnout will be most effective if six strategies are implemented to some degree, since each strategy addresses a different aspect of the burnout sequence. The relationship between the aspects and strategies is pictured in Table 1. To facilitate workshop planning, I have grouped activities under the strategy they most clearly implement.

TABLE 1

RELATIONSHIP BETWEEN ASPECTS OF BURNOUT SEQUENCE AND SIX PREVENTION STRATEGIES

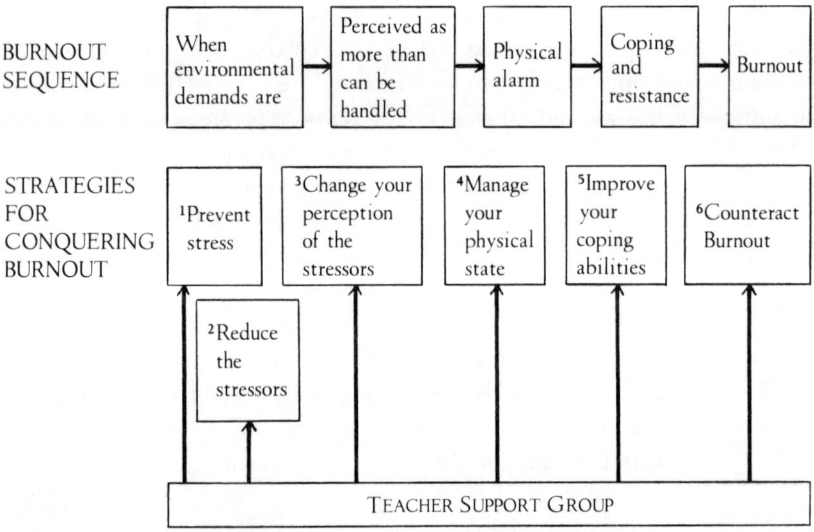

*This note constitutes permission by the National Education Association and Alfred Alschuler for unlimited photocopying of the workshop activities described in the following section.

1. Prevent stress.

To the degree that stressors continue in school, teachers must cope with them. The purpose of the following activities is to prevent teachers from experiencing excessive stress in order that they may devote their energies to teaching rather than to overcoming the obstacles to teaching.

Support Groups

Virtually all writers and fighters of burnout agree that support groups help prevent burnout and facilitate a wide range of other constructive activities. Support groups need not be complicated, lengthy, or formal. Two elements, however, are essential: a chance to express one's feelings (any feelings, positive or negative); and a chance to receive support (encouragement, a compliment, a warm fuzzy, a stroke, a hug, or a statement of appreciation). Support groups can be large and formal, such as a well attended workshop. They can also be small with only two people; and informal as, for example, two friends who car pool to work. Whether among professional colleagues or with a loved spouse or friend, there must be a sharing of feelings and some indication of support. This activity introduces the elements of support groups. It is an extended, formal version of the ten-minute dyads that begin each subsequent workshop session.

1. Each participant should complete the following inventory of burnout feelings.

How often do you experience these feelings in relation to your job?

	Never	Once	Rarely	Sometimes	Often	Usually	Always
1. Being tired	0	1	2	3	4	5	6
2. Feeling depressed	0	1	2	3	4	5	6
3. Having a bad day	0	1	2	3	4	5	6
4. Being physically exhausted	0	1	2	3	4	5	6
5. Being emotionally exhausted	0	1	2	3	4	5	6
6. Being wiped out	0	1	2	3	4	5	6
7. Feeling pushed around	0	1	2	3	4	5	6

	Never	Once	Rarely	Sometimes	Often	Usually	Always
8. Being unhappy	0	1	2	3	4	5	6
9. Feeling trapped or locked in	0	1	2	3	4	5	6
10. Feeling cynical	0	1	2	3	4	5	6
11. Feeling worthless	0	1	2	3	4	5	6
12. Wanting to quit	0	1	2	3	4	5	6
13. Being cold, callous, or hostile	0	1	2	3	4	5	6
14. Feeling disillusioned about people	0	1	2	3	4	5	6
15. Feeling bored	0	1	2	3	4	5	6
16. Feeling hopeless	0	1	2	3	4	5	6
17. Feeling resentful about people	0	1	2	3	4	5	6
18. Feeling pessimistic about outcomes	0	1	2	3	4	5	6
19. Feeling listless	0	1	2	3	4	5	6
20. Feeling anxious	0	1	2	3	4	5	6

Obtain your total score: [ ]

2. Divide into small groups of two, three, or four to discuss the meaning of your score, i.e., how you feel about your job. As a rough guideline, the scores may be divided into levels of Burnout:

0-60	Ideal
61-80	Mild Burnout
81-100	Moderate Burnout
101-120	Severe Burnout

In approximately twenty minutes make sure all participants have their scores.

3. In the same small group each person should express some kind of honest support or appreciation for every other member. This may be empathy for what the person has described, a compliment, or even an appreciation for something the person has felt but has never expressed. Take approximately ten minutes for this activity.
4. Return to the large group so that individuals may share their reactions to the previous half hour. It may be interesting also to discuss the location and frequency of sharing feelings and giving support in one's professional and personal lives. Infrequency of such behaviors is a major cause of burnout.

Friends in Need

All teachers know that stressors in their personal lives affect their feelings and performance at work. Too few schools provide any formal way to help teachers cope with the inevitable external crises. This activity begins by generating a comprehensive list of stressors in teachers' personal lives and then moves toward plans for mutual assistance.

1. Each participant should take five minutes to write down a list of all the stressors each one has experienced in the last 12 months. Here are some frequently mentioned stressors:

    Death of a loved one or friend
    Divorce
    Marital difficulties
    Personal injury or illness
    Injury or illness of a family member
    Marriage
    Pregnancy
    Sex difficulties
    New financial obligations
    Son or daughter leaving home
    Change of residence
    Change in recreation
    Change in sleeping habits
    Change in eating habits
    Returning from a vacation
    Minor violations of the law
    Equipment breakdowns

Check the items that have occurred in your life and add to this list any that may have been omitted.

2. Form groups of four to six. If you do not wish to discuss the specific stressors, at least describe how the stressor(s) affected your work, your feelings at work, your concentration, efficiency, effectiveness, and relationships with others. Take about 35 minutes for this activity.
3. Discuss the desirability and feasibility of creating "mutual assistance pacts," a "buddy system," or a teacher "hotline." If there is appropriate interest, make an agreement with another teacher to form such a pact.

Resource Network

Teachers' unusual talents are often hidden from public view, not by design, but because schools seldom survey the wide range of teacher expertise. Most specific problems can be solved by matching needs with existing expertise. The purpose of this session is to develop a visible resource network within your school and to begin the matching process. Any or all of the following activities can be helpful, depending on the time and degree of interest in the support group.

1. Go around the members of your group with each person describing her/his special talents or expertise, inside and outside school. Keep a list of these resources. Find out whether the teachers are willing to spend time sharing their skills with others if they receive something they need in return.
2. Augment this resource list with the expertise known by group members to be found among their colleagues in the school. Find out whether these individuals are willing to help.
3. Create an inventory of needs. Members of the group may want help from other members; post a list of the discovered talents with names and phone numbers so that other teachers may avail themselves of these resources (new teachers often have classroom management problems for which the hard-earned expertise of an older teacher is particularly relevant). Brainstorm a list of any other human resource needs that may exist in your school. Take turns describing a classroom problem; then let other teachers describe methods that have worked for them.

Teachers who join the resource network offering their talents are likely to find it easier to ask for help. Such a systematic method of cooperation can keep stressors from building up.

2. Reduce the stressors.

This strategy can be accomplished in two ways—by changing the stressful situation or by reducing one's exposure to the stressors, e.g., by job rotation through stressful situations; by sharing a contract with another teacher; by taking a "sick day," leave of absence, or sabbatical. The following activities concentrate on ways to reduce the stressors.

Conduct a Stress Hunt

This collaborative problem-solving activity is fully described earlier in this book in the chapter "Conquering Common Stressors."

Don't Say Yes When You Want to Say No

A book of this title authored by Fensterheim and Baer* is billed as "the assertiveness training book." One good way to reduce or prevent stress is to exercise one's innate right to say no to requests, i.e., stressors. Three chapters in the book are particularly relevant: 2. "Targeting Your Own Assertive Difficulties," 3. "The Assertion Laboratory," and 12. "Assertion on the Job." Each chapter has activities suitable for group work. Depending on the level of interest in the group, there is material for three or more sessions. One member could be selected for each chapter to guide the group through an assertiveness training program. A good way to make these plans is to assign a group member to review the book and then make a proposal during the evaluation and planning portion of a subsequent session.

Lighten the Load

The load you carry outside school has an effect on your burnout level in school. Just as it is useful to reduce stressors in school, this can be done elsewhere in your life with equally beneficial results. With your support group, conduct another stress hunt, this time for categories of stress *outside* school. The procedure is precisely the same as that outlined in "Conquering Common Stressors" in the second part of this book. After planning individual solutions, be sure to set dates to report to each other on your progress and problems. Your mutual assistance pacts can be useful in carrying out your plans.

**Don't Say Yes When You Want to Say No*, Herbert Fensterheim, Jean Baer (New York: Dell, 1975).

3. Change your perception of the stressors.

The major causes of teacher burnout are stressors in the school. Yet most of the solutions proposed in articles and workshops tell teachers what they should do to manage *their* thoughts, feelings, and actions. These proposals could be categorized as "victim, heal thyself." To win the war on stress the first targets are the stressors—too many discipline problems and too little pay, too much paperwork and not enough supplies or community support, . . . etc. Such stressors should be reduced and burnout should be prevented.

In addition to the collaborative efforts required to make schools more habitable and healthy, teachers can also employ strategies to prevent the pain of victimization, and to maintain commitment and effectiveness.

The first of these teacher-centered strategies involves managing one's perception of the stressor. This strategy exploits the obvious human freedom of perception. For instance, one day a petty bureaucratic request is simply another thing to do. The next day it is infuriating. The third day the same request is merely absurd. Deliberately changing one's perception can change one's response from anger to hilarity, from frustration to challenge, from smoldering resentment to stoicism. Regardless of the toxicity of the situation, teachers should not have to suffer and carry toxic responses. Here are some ways to manage your perceptions.

Put Things into Perspective

Most teachers keep lists of things they must do. It's a survival technique. Some feel oppressed by such lists and what they don't accomplish. This exercise is designed to keep lists in proper perspective. *First*, take five minutes to make out a list of things to do, in your normal way. *Second*, in order to put lists into perspective, one must have a clear perspective. Take three minutes (and only three) to make a new list of all those things you want to have, be, or do three years from now. Don't censure your thoughts. Write down everything that occurs to you. Then take another three minutes to review your list, checking to see whether anything important was not included.

Third, prioritize your list by assigning an A, B, or C to each item: "A" refers to any item on your "to do" list clearly related to one or more of your three-year goals; "B" refers to items that *must* be done today in order to avoid consequences you do not wish to bear; "C" refers to items that can be postponed one day, or those with consequences for omission you are willing to take for a day.

Fourth, analyze your list using the following guidelines: (1) *always* have at least one "A" item on every "to do" list; (2) *never* do a "C" item until it becomes a "B"; (3) check for the "80:20 rule" (if you were to asterisk 20 percent of the most important items, do they include 80 percent of those most important to accomplish that day?).

In small groups take some time to raise questions or to discuss any discoveries made during this exercise. Here are two additional comments to consider.

1. Some people play a failure game that goes like this. Before each day begins they make an optimistic list of absolutely everything they want to accomplish that day. They try hard, but, inevitably, do not complete the list. Then, instead of setting more moderate goals for the next day or prioritizing the list, or congratulating themselves for how much they did accomplish, they choose to see the incompleted list as a catalog of their failures. Do you play some variation of this failure game?
2. Some teachers often complain there is never time for an "A" item. Let's assume this is true. Are you willing to give up all your "A" goals? What are you willing to give up? All goals are attained by making certain sacrifices. What are you willing to sacrifice for your goals?

Victimization and Choice

School days may seem synonymous with a pawnlike existence—being controlled by bells and regulations, paperwork that cannot be done in the time allowed, students making legitimate but impossible requests. After months of this daily routine, the feelings of powerlessness, lack of freedom, and being treated by the system like a child who must be controlled—all these feelings can intensify irritations with the chores. This exercise explores the issue of the degree to which teachers are pawns victimized by the system.

Step 1: Divide into pairs. Taking turns, choose a situation in school in which you were completely victimized. Take about five minutes to persuade the other person that you had absolutely *no* choice in the matter, you did not set it up or allow it to continue, and could not control the consequences. During this explanation the other person is not to say anything, or ask questions, or agree or disagree. When you are finished making your case, find out whether the listener agrees that you were *completely* victimized.

Step 2: Take the other side. For up to five minutes, explore all the places where you did either set it up, allow it to continue, or choose to see yourself as a victim. What choices were made by committing yourself to an action, by omitting action, or by the way you chose to interpret the situation?

Steps 3 and 4: Repeat steps 1 and 2, exchanging roles.

After completing step 4, it may be helpful to share insights in the large group. Teachers cannot always control what the school demands of them, confronts them with, or prohibits. Like all human beings, however, teachers do control their responses. They can also manage their perceptions. Did teachers in the group discover specific new ways to perceive, to feel and act less like a victim?

4. Manage your physical state.

Whatever the cause, once stress is experienced, there are important immediate physiological consequences and serious potential long-term hazards. Teachers can intervene directly by managing their physical tensions, by regulating the body's chemical reactions (e.g., cutting out processed sugar, caffeine, and alcohol), and even by controlling their brain waves.

Relax Without Drugs

The chapter by Benson earlier in this book provides complete instructions for achieving the relaxation response. Have the leader of one session conduct participants on a guided tour to the relaxation response. After 15 to 20 minutes in the relaxed state, group members may want to talk about how they felt, when it is possible to use this technique, and its application (for example, how it can help people fall asleep at night). Teachers in the group who have had practice with different types of meditation will be able to describe other alternatives and the long-term effects of regular relaxation/meditation.

Control Your Body's Vibrations

Virtually all the bodily processes have an electrical aspect. Stages of meditation and sleep are reflected in alpha, gamma, and delta brain wave patterns; tension levels are reflected in one's galvanic skin response (GSR) and in muscle tension. Certain machines measure these electrical patterns and translate them into variable pitch sounds so that it is possible, for example, to hear changes in one's tension level (GSR). More than the novelty of listening to the body, it is possible to learn how to control these physical states by learning to change the sounds. You can learn to relax, control your heart rate and pulse, raise your skin temperature, turn on alpha brain wave patterns, etc. All that is required is a "biofeedback machine," a device that translates *bio*logical vibrations into auditory *feedback*, i.e., sound. Although there are many devices on the market today for as little as $100 to $200, they are limited and can be unreliable. More importantly, they do not come with an instructor who will donate an hour or two. The most likely places to find them are in the departments of psychology, physical education, or health sciences of the nearest college or university. Certain hospitals and clinics also may have these machines. The possibilities for this new field extend beyond lie detecting, curing headaches, and teaching alpha meditation. The range of applications and local opportunities to learn how to turn on electrically are best known to a local expert. See what the nearest expert would be willing to do for your group. Typically, these training sessions are fascinating, useful, fun, and well worth the time spent in making the arrangements.

5. Improve your coping abilities.

In the long haul, effective daily functioning is based on a repertoire of high-level skills. When a needed skill is lacking, stress is intensified. It would be useful for the support group to create an inventory of needed skills and then arrange for specific training. Often this can be done without cost. For instance, when a Massachusetts law mandated the mainstreaming of students with special needs, many teachers needed new skills. In several schools this need was met by special education teachers in the schools during in-service education days. Some other examples of coping skills follow.

Manage Your Time Better

Earlier in this book Lakein suggested 20 ways to get control of your time and your life. These techniques were intended for a general audience, not only teachers. In each support group there is a hidden list of at least 20 tricks for saving time inside and outside school. Go around the group asking each person to give a favorite time-saving technique. Continue until all the techniques are out, being sure to have someone write them down. After generating the list, take a few minutes for each person to look for one, two, or three specific personal applications. Then, spend some time discussing the problems and possibilities for saving time.

Has Anyone Caught the "Frenzies"?

When teachers try too hard to get more and more done in less and less time, they can become frenzied. When sprinting becomes a lifestyle, teachers exhibit other symptoms of the frenzies, or, in more technical terms, "Type A behavior." In the short run it may be productive to be a work demon. However, the long-term consequences may be too severe. People with Type A behavior are three times more likely to have a coronary "accident." Short of a heart attack, frenzied teachers are racing toward burnout. One good way to begin preventing these serious problems is to diagnose frenzy early and to intervene.

1. Using Friedman and Rosenman's criteria for Type A behavior, each person in the group should do a self-assessment and assess one other person outside the group who is a candidate for frenzy. If you have doubts about your own diagnosis, ask other members of the group.
2. Discuss alternative ways of sharing your concern with frenzied individuals, and helping them move toward a safer lifestyle. There may be reluctance to "interfere" with another person's lifestyle, or even comment on it, unasked. On the other hand, it is not responsible to ignore dangers obvious to you and unseen by others. The advantages and disadvantages of acting and not acting need to be weighed carefully. The support group is helpful in this process. Whatever is done, or not done, should be reported to the group so that all may learn from each person's experience.
3. It will not have escaped your attention that teachers who use time too inefficiently get swamped, while those who try to cram too much into the available time may be heading for trouble of a different kind. A happy medium for one person may differ from a happy medium for another. It may be useful to discuss in small groups the following questions: How efficient are you willing to become? How many tasks are you willing to postpone? What deadlines are you willing to miss?

6. Counteract burnout.

Everyone needs a safe haven, if not a place, then a time and an activity that guarantee a respite from stress. Glasser describes such havens as "positive addictions." Whether called "hobbies," "diversions," or "messing around," they are more than benign, they are necessary "goals." Most people have a favorite "escape" and are willing to advertise it. It may be useful and interesting in one group session for participants to boast about the virtues of their positive addictions. If you don't have one, you may get a few ideas. This innocent sharing activity also has unexpected benefits: You will see some surprising sides of people, you will learn of more expertise available in a crunch, and you may discover new ways to make your positive addiction more positive and more addicting.

WORKSHOP ROLES*

A support group may involve three of four teachers in a school who meet regularly, or the entire faculty of a school system during a one-day, in-service workshop. The setting, purpose, membership, and frequency of support group meetings vary widely. Regardless of the particular situation, there are three basic roles: the initiator (a teacher, counselor, principal, assistant superintendent in charge of in-service education, professor of education, etc.); the workshop session leader; and participants. The recommendations for each role which follow may be excessive. If you think a recommendation is inappropriate or unnecessary for your situation, modify or ignore it.

How to Begin: Notes to the Initiator

Several people may be enticed by the idea of a support group, or perhaps you are a sole, curious reader toying with the notion of organizing a group. No matter how the group begins, one person generally takes responsibility for getting it started.

As the initiator, your first task is to learn enough about the material to recruit other group members by convincing them that these experiences may meet their needs. When you begin recruiting within a school system, consider members of the administration. Often they can supply incentives such as in-service credit; tangible help like money for books and resources; and the essential, intangible help of their own enthusiasm. Encourage members of the administration to participate. If they work alongside teachers, you will have a doubly effective group. Moreover, the exercises and discussions that occur in the group about stress, discipline, teaching styles, and classroom and school situations will be valuable, shared experiences.

---

*This material is adapted from *Teaching Achievement Motivation* by Alschuler, Tabor, and McIntyre (Middletown, Conn.: Education Ventures, Inc., 1970).

Ideally, the total support group can include three to thirty or more persons who have volunteered because of special interest and favorable impressions from your advance information. The group should be small enough to work in a close, straightforward way over a period of time. Thus, more than fifteen participants should split into subgroups to facilitate interaction. In these working groups there should be a mix of men and women, with a variety of subject matter specializations, talents, ethnic backgrounds, personality types, and ages. Such composition makes for a richer exchange of ideas. An already formed group, however, such as members of the guidance or physical education or social studies departments, may also decide to form a group. In this case there is the advantage of a common focus on content, problems, and teaching styles and a greater chance for effectively implementing new ideas.

Group meetings can vary in length, just as the number of meetings can multiply, depending on the direction the group takes and the involvement members feel. Various schedules are possible—from long weekend retreats (Thursday evening through Sunday evening), to a series of weekly meetings, or some combination of the two. It may be useful to present these alternative schedules to people so that they will know how much time will be required. A definite schedule can wait until the first meeting, when the group can make a joint decision about the time and location of future meetings.

Let us assume that you have progressed through the sequence just described: you have read this book, and perhaps the administration is receptive to the idea of allowing teachers some released time and in-service credit for tackling this independent project. Several teachers are interested in the group and are willing to devote time. You have scouted out room possibilities and invited all who are interested to an hour-long introductory meeting. The purposes of the meeting are to help interested teachers decide whether to participate in the group and to make plans for getting under way.

A list of goals and guidelines follows. The list is a contribution to a pool of topics and issues from which you can draw to create a first meeting that will accomplish your own goals.

1. Set a tone and an atmosphere that are comfortable and evocative. The group has natural selling points. People have found it fun, interesting, and worthwhile. Avoid creating pressure. Create conditions that make people want to accept an invitation (e.g., describe a sample exercise, or have the principal express enthusiasm).
2. Give a brief sketch of the background, rationale, and potential benefits of a support group.

3. Discuss what the group can accomplish: reducing stress in the classroom, school, and personal life; providing interpersonal and emotional support; raising consciousness about how to resolve conflict; and making schools an easier place in which to love.
4. Indicate what the group is like. Try to convey the experiential, relaxed, participatory climate. Give examples of the contents: role plays, games, exercises, discussions. Explain how the course will be run. If this is a group of teachers, there will not be an instructor; instead everyone will share the leadership role by taking turns for each session.
5. Be prepared to consider questions about housekeeping details such as the following: Is anyone taking overall responsibility? Who will lead each session? Where will it be? What is the schedule for the group? Will any credit or compensation be given? If it is a university course, students may want to know what is required to pass. These housekeeping details can be handled in a short follow-up meeting by those people who decide to join the group. It is important to assign leaders for the first two sessions so that everyone has ample time to prepare.
6. Decide on the focus of the first session or two. Take the strategies described in the first part of this guide as a sequence of objectives, choosing activities within each strategy.

How to Lead a Session: Notes to the Facilitator

When leading a session, your assignments will range from mundane assembling of materials to the subtle creation of a tone and an atmosphere that help the session click. You must perform some duties yourself, while the group shares other duties with you. More specifically, let's consider your role as a three-stage process: planning the session, guiding the session, and leading the evaluation at the end of the session.

Planning the Session

Before the session, you are like a production manager responsible for staging. The following types of preparation will help the production come off successfully.

1. Plan your session far enough in advance to tell participants about any reading they should do beforehand.
2. Understand the game or experiment directions so that you can clarify the objectives and sequence of activities for the group and keep the session from bogging down in details.

3. Make some arrangements for refreshments, if appropriate. Provide for the comfort of the group. As a minimum, have a break halfway through the session.
4. See that any necessary materials are available and properly set up before the session begins.

An important ingredient for the success of any session is an enthusiastic, open-minded attitude. When you are the leader, accept the fact that you can prepare only up to a point. You are not going to be the teacher leading the class in lockstep through an outlined plan of the day. You will be more like a director who has set the stage for the activity about to begin. After careful preparation, relax and breathe deeply. (Physiologically, taking enormous breaths is one of the best ways to relieve tension.)

Guiding the Session

Begin the session by briefly explaining the purpose, writing the two or three objectives on the board, and describing the sequence and approximate time periods for the activities. Don't forget to start the session with a ten-minute minisupport group in which individuals in pairs each take five minutes to express feelings and get positive feedback of any kind. Run the major exercise or activity efficiently, allowing ample time for discussion, but do not be so glued to the schedule that you are seen as a drill sergeant. Rather, try to be attentive to people's involvement and enjoyment. Careful advance preparation and a certain amount of agility will carry you gracefully through the mechanics of the activity. Try to move to each succeeding step shortly after energy has peaked, not when the group is exhausted.

As discussion leader, you will be working with everyone else to gain insights. Consequently, you will be called upon to "play it by ear" a good deal of the time. From prior reading, you should be ready with questions to stimulate the group's thinking. But be prepared to modify, or even discard, parts of your plan. There is an important distinction between preparation and planning. Adequate preparation will help you use your knowledge to facilitate the group's functioning. It will help you improvise on where the group has decided to take the discussion. Planning that is too specific is likely to cause resistance. The real skill of the discussion leader is to make whatever happens in the situation relevant to participants' concerns.

Besides helping the group accomplish its goals, you must also accept responsibility for "group maintenance" and be watchful of the *group process*:

How is the task being carried out? What are the interactions in the group? Is everyone contributing? If not, why not? Are people apathetic, angry, distracted? For example, if one person constantly digresses or dominates the group, it affects everyone and is a matter of group concern. To tolerate this under the pretext of "getting on with the job" will impair the group's functioning. Usually the best time to take up and resolve these interpersonal issues is during the evaluation period of the session.

In any group, personal energy can manifest itself in defensive, destructive behavior or in supportive, productive behavior. Progress on group tasks is contingent on good working relationships among participants—including ideally an openness, trust, and support. Everyone should feel responsible for creating this working atmosphere, but you in particular can contribute most to such a climate by practicing the following specific leadership behaviors.

1. Listen superbly, and encourage the rest of the group to do the same. A good way to check how well you are listening is to see if you can paraphrase to yourself the speaker's comments.
2. Never compete with members of the group or struggle to have your own ideas heard. As leader, you are present for *their* benefit. Later, as a follower, you can attend to your concerns. As leader, remember that the best rule of thumb is to hold off your comments until everyone else has finished. Often, others will make your point and feel good about contributing.
3. Use every member of the group. This means inviting participation of the shy or reluctant (with eye contact or perhaps a nod of the head) and tactfully suggesting some boundaries for those who tend to dominate the group ("Thank you, I've got the idea.").
4. Intervene in the ways that clarify what has happened. When the time feels right, paraphrase what has been going on and what has been said. Identify points of confusion and questions that seem to be left hanging. You need not resolve the confusion yourself. For example, you might say, "Could someone summarize the alternatives that have been mentioned so far?" or "I'm not sure I understood your last point—could you say a little more?" or "Could someone else give me an understanding of what was said?"
5. Help members develop the habit of personalizing comments, especially those that affect other group members. Help people take responsibility rather than blame others. For example, another way for a participant to say "You monopolize the group" is to say "I would like to talk more, but

I find it very uncomfortable trying to stop you." The second remark is fairer, because the person addressed can stop talking graciously without losing face and feeling attacked. Further, encourage people to avoid making comments to no one in particular. Often it is helpful to say something like "Can you address that comment to a specific person?"

6. Prevent anyone from being "put down." Help the group be positive by stressing the value of ideas and comments, not the potential pitfall. First, say what it is you like about a person's idea, no matter how bad it is; then say what concerns you. This procedure recognizes that people will disagree, but also that good ideas are often lost because people are not willing to look at them carefully.
7. Try to be a "barometer" for the group. If you feel tension vibrating around people, express that feeling. Depending on your own sense of the situation, your own style and inclination, the expression might be humorous or perfectly straight, but it should open the possibility of talking about what is wrong and relieving people's feelings. Conversely, if people are really tuned in and enjoying themselves, join in. Help sustain the mood.
8. Keep the pace energetic and lively. You are accustomed to working with groups of students and you know that the energy level and involvement of a group often mirrors your own energy for the day. If you are alert and involved, the group is more likely to be enthusiastic and interested. Start on time and aim to finish at a given time. Avoid the kind of laissez-faire leadership that lets a group languish and then forces everyone to catch up madly by being stingy with time later. You can decide when to push and move people on, when to let the group settle down to relax or hassle over a point. People may well look to you to indicate when to break a silence or when to allow for time to think and feel. Or they may need the relief of hearing you say, "We've been working pretty hard; let's take a break." This kind of pacing depends particularly on the leader of the session.

Evaluating the Session

During the evaluation phase of the session, members of the group as a whole consider how they are doing in terms of the following:

1. Learning about solutions to stress
2. The effectiveness of the session just concluded
3. Working relationships and cooperation within the group.

The evaluation is not simply an evaluation of the leader as such, nor is it a final comment on a finished product. Instead, it is more like the process of steering a boat. The end point is known, but the winds, tide, and current all necessitate constant adjustment and attention to steering. Allow enough time for people to fill out the form, discuss the results, and make plans. Fifteen to twenty minutes is usually enough. A series of simple hand counts can summarize the numerical aspects of the evaluation. Another five to ten minutes to discuss the evaluation results will be helpful to the group and to the leader of the next session. When the agreed-upon stopping time has been reached, a useful way to obtain closure and a summary is to "go around." Have each person in the group complete one of the following sentence stems: "What I found most interesting today was . . ." or "What I learned today was . . ." or "The most useful thing I learned today was. . . ." Then, present your own two- to four-minute summary of the session, reviewing the objectives, the actions taken to reach those objectives, the key concepts, and general conclusions. It may be useful to prepare part of this summary during your planning before the session.

Any group engaged in a long-term project experiences a range of success. There will be some periods when people are less involved than at others, and sessions where conflict is unavoidable. On some days the feeling will be one of enjoyment and accomplishment. Accept the highs and the lows in a way that allows you to learn from both extremes. Careful attention to the evaluation process will help you do so. As facilitator, you will be responsible for engaging the group in the evaluation activity and organizing the comments into a useful form that can be passed on to the next leader.

Your final task is to ensure the continuity of the group. Is there agreement on the purpose and activity for the next session? Has the facilitator been chosen? Make sure your successor receives all the evaluation forms to study. Does everyone know the time, place, and preparation (if any)?

How to Participate in the Support Group: Notes to Members

Your group will be unique. No one of you can be sure what will happen. The combination of personalities, the decisions made along the way, the special goals, the room you work in, a dozen quirks and circumstances will make your group unlike any other.

The directions for the group do not constitute a syllabus. They are more like the outline of a play or the road map of a country open for exploration. This description may appeal to your sense of adventure and at the same time make you a bit nervous. "How," you may ask, "will I know when I've reached the objectives?" Since there is no "expert," you will have to help each other in at least three ways. First, prepare extremely well for the session you lead because during that session you are the "expert" for the other workshop members. Second, during the session keep the critical problem-solving sequence in mind. It will allow you to anticipate what will happen and help you coordinate your contributions more effectively. Third, at the end of every session, during the scheduled evaluation period, give frank, specific feedback about how the session went and what can be improved during the next sesion. This advice is as important for others before they lead as it will be for you in preparing to lead your session.

Support Group Evaluation

The purposes of this questionnaire are to help the group improve its functioning and to provide the leader of the next session with specific suggestions.

	Poor		Fair		Good		Very Good			Excellent
1. Overall, how would you rate today's session? (Circle one)	1	2	3	4	5	6	7	8	9	10
2. How valuable was today's session?	1	2	3	4	5	6	7	8	9	10
3. How interested are you in the techniques and concepts you learned today?	1	2	3	4	5	6	7	8	9	10
4. How well were the stated objectives met?	1	2	3	4	5	6	7	8	9	10

5. Please indicate your degree of satisfaction with each of the following aspects of the session:

	Unsatisfied	*OK*	*Very Satisfied*
Clarity of the objectives	___	___	___
Clarity of directions and examples	___	___	___
Relevance of daily problems	___	___	___
Work done in small groups	___	___	___
Pace: neither too fast nor too slow	___	___	___
Validation of individuals	___	___	___
Warm, conducive learning climate	___	___	___
Clarity of the summary	___	___	___

6. In order to improve the group's functioning in the next session:
   (a) What good aspects of this session should be continued?
   (b) What aspects should be changed? How?

ANNOTATED BIBLIOGRAPHY OF USEFUL BOOKS ABOUT STRESS

Boyd Swent and Walter Gmelch

Ardell, Donald D. *High Level Wellness*. Emmaus, PA: Rodale Press, 1977.

High Level Wellness represents one of the best resource books available to help people find an alternative to doctors, drugs, and diseases. Wellness, as contrasted with illness, is much more than the absence of disease but the reinforcement of health-enhancing behaviors in the areas of nutrition, physical fitness, environmental sensitivity, self-responsibility, and stress management. Ardell, therefore, does not believe there is a single cause of wellness or illness. He has come to realize that wellness consists of many positive practices which should be used harmoniously. Living up to this theme, the author provides us with a wealth of resource materials from addresses and contacts at Wellness Centers, guidelines for wellness, self-assessment instruments, to an extensive annotated bibliography of major books within each of the five wellness areas. *High Level Wellness* is a must for those wishing to embark on a multi-faceted and well balanced attack on stress.

Dudley, Donald L., and Welke, Elton. *How to Survive Being Alive*. Garden City, N.Y.: Doubleday and Co., 1977.

Much of this book is based on the exploration of stress, disease, and the impact of life changes. The authors dispel the ancient distinction between physical diseases and mental diseases. This separate treatment may be, as the authors point out, the single greatest deterrent to quality health care in our country. While the authors spend considerable time elaborating on the complex disease profiles of angina pectoris, myocardial infarction, vasovagal fainting, ulcerative colitis . . . they do pose an intriguing strategy for coping with stress: avoid the great swings from

---

Excerpted from *Stress at the Desk and How to Cope Creatively* by Boyd Swent and Walter Gmelch, Oregon School Study Council Bulletin 21, no. 4 (December 1977), School of Education, University of Oregon, Eugene. Reprinted with permission.

activity to inactivity by maintaining a steady level of productive activity at work and play. Slowing down and gearing up should be accomplished in mild degrees rather than moving from "the thrill of victory" to the "agony of defeat."

Funkenstein, Daniel H.; King, Stanley H.; and Drolette, Margaret. *Mastery of Stress*. Cambridge: Harvard University Press, 1957.

Mastery of Stress reports a series of experiments conducted with a group of college men at Harvard University over a period of two years. Although technical in nature, this book elaborates on how people react to certain new and difficult situations. The authors advance the theory that acute emergency reactions represent an innate aspect of the personality (defense mechanisms in the initial stages), whereas the mastery of stress results from total life experiences (the ability to cope). In seeking and understanding the so-called diseases of stress, they postulate that it is important to study three phases of stress reactions: (1) the acute emergency reaction (fight or flight), (2) the ability to handle stress as time passes (coping mechanisms), and (3) the sustained or chronic stress reaction.

Gmelch, Walter H. *Beyond Stress to Effective Management*. Eugene, Oregon: Oregon School Study Council Bulletin, Vol. 20, nos. 9 and 10, 1977.

This monograph deals with the subject of stress—what it is, its sources and causes, the variety of human responses to stress, its consequences, and how to cope with stress. Although the booklet is addressed to school administrators in particular, its prescriptions have value for individuals in all fields and at all levels. It provides checklists to identify one's own sources of stress and provides suggestions from a variety of sources on how to cope with various kinds of stress. The author offers four "stress absorbers" to take the shock out of stress for the school manager: (1) know the limitations of administration (and administrators), (2) establish and update life goals, (3) develop the ability to relax as quickly and completely as possible, and (4) develop a "holistic" approach to stress—both the mind and body must work together to reduce stress. A checklist to score one's own ability to relax is included, as is a bibliography on stress and related topics. (Annotation provided by Educational Research Service Bulletin, September 1977.)

Lamott, Kenneth. *Escape from Stress*. New York: Berkeley Medallion Books, 1974.

Kenneth Lamott succinctly summarizes some of the major diseases of stress: hypertension, heart attack, cancer, aging, ulcers, and other physiological disorders. While speaking to the relationship between stress and disease, he rightfully criticizes people for always looking to science for the cure when the cure is really within ourselves. Disease is not caused by a germ but by a change in our relationship to that germ. Most of his book deals with escaping from stress through letting go with meditation, hypnosis, and biofeedback. Although these meditative devices are helpful mechanisms for coping with stress, readers should be cautioned that this is only one approach and should be balanced with others such as proper nutrition, physical fitness, positive philosophies of life, and effective management techniques.

Mackenzie, R. Alec. *The Time Trap*. New York: McGraw-Hill, 1975.

We all have exactly the same amount of time, but 90 percent of the managers complain that they never have enough. *The Time Trap*, a study of timewasters, suggests ways out of the trap. Drawing upon his years of business management experience, Mackenzie shares a number of simple, straightforward and applicable ideas for handling such time and stress traps as procrastination, constant interruptions, the open-door, corridor wanderers, continuous meetings, and lack of organization, planning and setting priorities. His book should be read with the idea that it presents a smorgasbord of insightful tips and techniques on how to better manage your time: from his spread of wares you are free to sample techniques which suit your taste. *The Time Trap* is a book you will want available on your reference shelf to help you cope with the stresses of time.

McQuade, Walter, and Aikman, Ann. *Stress*. New York: Bantam Books, 1974.

McQuade and Aikman's well-documented book—prompted by the authors' award winning article in *Fortune* magazine—examines what stress can do to your cardiovascular, digestive, skeletal-muscular, and immunitive systems and provides insight into how the mind and body handle stress (and how the mind sometimes "betrays" the body!). The final and most substantial portion of the book provides the reader with personal solutions for stress reduction including diet, exercise, psychotherapy, encounter groups, meditation, biofeedback, drugs, and hypnotism. While this single book is a necessity, it represents only a beginning. The authors provide a brief list of annotated readings for further investigation.

Pelletier, Kenneth R. *Mind as Healer, Mind as Slayer*. New York: Dell Publishing Co., 1977.

Dr. Pelletier approaches stress from a holistic point of view; that is the mind, body, and spirit must work together in harmony to prevent stress disorders. *Mind as Healer, Mind as Slayer* surveys the sources of stress, provides a guideline for the evaluation of stress levels, reports research on profiles of stress-prone personalities, and concludes with a practical section on preventing stress-related diseases through meditation, biofeedback and autogenic training, and visualization. As Gay Luce has pointed out, using this book is as important as reading it.

Selye, Hans. *The Stress of Life*. New York: McGraw-Hill, 1976.

The Stress of Life, first published in 1956 and revised, expanded, and updated with new research findings in 1976, continues to provide a summary of the contemporary scientific basis of the entire stress concept. Selye does not intend this to be an "inspirational book" where readers blindly believe in his statements. His intent is to enable the educated nonmedical readers to make up their own minds about the validity of laboratory experiences to everyday problems. The book proceeds from the discovery of stress to the analysis of its mechanism in health and disease; then explores how this knowledge could further our understanding of how to face stress. While Selye's intention is to reach the nontechnical reader, his dispersing of highly technical data between the more easily readable and entertaining parts of his narrative makes the book cumbersome to read. For those who are less familiar with many of the stress-related concepts and terminology, "Book IV" provides practical implications and applications of stress concepts to everyday life. Selye's suggestions in this part are based upon devising a healthy philosophy of life primarily rooted in "altruistic egoism" which maximizes eustress (good stress) and minimizes distress (bad stress) in our lives. Even though technical (glossary of terms provided) *The Stress of Life* is essential reading for anyone seriously interested in the subject.

Selye, Hans. *Stress Without Distress*. New York: Signet Books, 1975.

"Stress is the spice of life," notes Dr. Hans Selye. In this classic, Selye describes the nature of stress, the triphasic general adaption syndrome, and what stress is and is not. While using scientific inquiry to base the first portion of his book, the latter chapters philosophically discuss the relationship between stress and "aims in life." His scientific pedigree is impeccable; however, his philosophical thoughts on stress reduction through "altruistic egoism," and "earn my neighbor's love," should be read as critically as the "how-to" books by Wayne Dyer, Albert Ellis, Eric Berne, and others who have just as much right to forward their philosophical answers to the stresses of life as does Selye.

Winter, Ruth. *Triumph over Tension*. New York: Grosset and Dunlap, 1976.

Triumph over Tension resembles many of the pop-psychology pieces we find in bookstores today. However, the author does provide some practical tips for learning to love leisure, how to take a real vacation, exercising for relaxation, and developing everyday coping techniques. Although many of the techniques suggested are self-evident, many times we need to be reminded more than instructed. A sampling of these techniques include suggestions to do something for others, arrange for privacy, don't insist on winning, own up to who you are, don't judge yourself sternly, get sufficient sleep, respect your body, change your environment, change your routine, talk to a friend, choose your associates carefully, find your stress level, learn to live for today, and seek a sense of humor.

Stress. Chicago: Blue Print for Health/Blue Cross Association, 1974.

A "freebie" from your local Blue Cross agency, this booklet assembles articles from many noted medical scholars. Not only are the authors knowledgeable on their subjects, but talented at presenting information clearly for the average reader. The articles cover stress at childhood, adolescence, and aging, as well as stress in the home, on the job, and in the environment. The booklet concludes with a chapter on learning how to relax.